Praise for *No Fear Networking*

"This book is for anyone who wants to get better at creating genuine connections with others, not just 'network' in a gross, transactional way."

—Ann Handley, Chief Content Officer, MarketingProfs;
Wall Street Journal **bestselling author of** *Everybody Writes*

"*No Fear Networking* is a guide to building connections without the overwhelm. Michaela Alexis shares practical, no-nonsense advice that helps people step out of their comfort zone and create real, lasting relationships."

—John Hall, Chief Advisor, Relevance.com; Co-founder
of Calendar.com; bestselling author of *Top of Mind*

"Have you ever walked into a room full of strangers, expected to network, only to feel your stomach tie itself in knots? Fear not! Michaela Alexis's *No Fear Networking* is the recipe for success you've been craving. I've watched Michaela rise from battling social anxiety to inspiring others, and this book serves up a feast of wisdom garnished with personal anecdotes and expert insights. What sets it apart is Michaela's real-world tested advice. It's not just theory – it's a proven recipe for networking success that will help you cook up meaningful connections and watch your career rise like a perfect soufflé."

—Phil Mershon, Director of Experience, Social Media Examiner;
event coach and speaker; bestselling author of *Unforgettable*

"Social anxiety isn't a one-size-fits-all disorder; it's a spectrum. For some, it's a nagging discomfort. For others, it's a debilitating fear that locks you in place. This book is for those who want to navigate that spectrum and find strategies that work, not to eliminate anxiety but to coexist with it."

—Swish Goswami, serial entrepreneur;
author of *The Young Entrepreneur*

"Concerned about rejection? Learn to put aside your fears with Michaela's book. You'll discover how to open lots of doors and secure a much brighter future!"

—Michael Stelzner, Founder, Social Media Examiner
and Social Media Marketing World

No Fear Networking

No Fear Networking

A Guide to
Building
Connections

FOR THE
SOCiALLY
ANXiOUS
PROFESSiONAL

MICHAELA ALEXIS

WILEY

Published by John Wiley & Sons, Inc., Hoboken, New Jersey.
Published simultaneously in Canada.

For general information on our other products and services or for technical support, please contact our Customer Care Department within the United States at (800) 762-2974, outside the United States at (317) 572-3993 or fax (317) 572-4002.

Wiley also publishes its books in a variety of electronic formats. Some content that appears in print may not be available in electronic formats. For more information about Wiley products, visit our web site at www.wiley.com.

Library of Congress Cataloging-in-Publication Data is Available:

ISBN 9781394268559 (Cloth)
ISBN 9781394268556 (ePub)
ISBN 9781394268573 (ePDF)

COVER DESIGN: PAUL MCCARTHY
COVER ART: © GETTY IMAGES: MARBLE
BACKGROUND: MEDINA CREATIVES
BOOK: EKATERINA GONCHAROVA

SKY10093701_121224

*To my dad, passed but forever present in every word
I write — I did it. I hope I've made you proud.*

*To my mom, you are forever my compass. You taught me not only
the power of words but also the power of the human spirit. You've
shaped me, pushed me, encouraged me, and always saw something
in me, even in times when I couldn't see it in myself.*

*And to Isla, my sweet little girl, you inspire me to reach
higher and dream bigger. This book is for you, a reminder
that you can do and be anything if you're brave enough
to face the wilderness and chase your dreams.*

Contents

Introduction

"What if an emergency happened right now and you couldn't escape?"

There I was, a 20-something-year-old wedged among fellow students in a vast lecture hall. The professor's monotonous voice filled the air, discussing the looming final exam. A sudden, unsettling thought hijacked my focus. I attempted to shrug it off, redirecting my attention to my laptop, desperate to jot down any crucial information about the upcoming test.

But the ambiance was shifting. Every minor sound amplified – the foot tapping from my left, the whispers and subdued laughter from my right.

My heartbeat accelerated, morphing these noises into a buzzing alarm that rang in my ears. I tried to ignore it, turning back toward my laptop as I attempted to capture any important details.

Suddenly, every sound became heightened around me. The student to my left tapping their foot. The one to my right whispering to a friend and giggling.

My heart started beating more quickly, and suddenly the sounds turned into ringing in my ears. A prickling sensation crept over my fingers; beads of sweat trailed down my chest. The room felt unbearably warm.

A new, alarming thought intruded, shattering my composure. *Could this be a heart attack?*

In a frantic scramble, I packed away my laptop, muttered apologies as I navigated through a sea of bored students, and made my escape.

I dashed toward the lecture hall's exit. Bursting through the doors, I headed straight for the sanctuary of the bathroom, locking myself in a stall.

Collapsing to the floor, chest tight and tears streaming, I was overcome by something I had never felt before: my first anxiety attack – a pivotal encounter with social anxiety that marked the beginning of what would become my new normal for decades to come.

I slowly became increasingly worried that the same thing would happen again, and I began to retreat more and more into the comfort of my own home. Eventually it got to the point where I would have to pump myself up as if I was going onto a sports field just to leave my house.

When I felt I had strayed too far from safety, I would have another panic attack and become overcome with nausea and dizziness. Soon, I became a prisoner of what I now know was agoraphobia.

I had to quit my job at the grocery store down the street. I stopped being able to dine in restaurants or take in a screening at a movie theater. I tried to visit theme parks and became sick within minutes of standing in a crowd.

I wasn't just struggling with anxiety; my life was overtaken by it.

Perhaps most stressful of all was that I was unable to make it all the way to school anymore because I couldn't get past the first stop on the train before having an anxiety attack and needing to get off. How would I ever be able to graduate if I couldn't even make it to campus for class?

Thankfully, many of my courses were available on demand via video recordings, so I was able to squeeze by until exam season. I studied for weeks, learning every speck of information I could memorize. I was ready. I was going to finally make it on campus and into the exam hall.

I walked to the train station, clutching my notes, determined to board. But when I got to the first station after boarding, the faces surrounding me started to become fuzzy. The train, which should have been swaying gently side to side, started spinning violently.

I felt queasy. I turned toward the open door, ready to flee again.

"What is the worst thing that can happen?" I heard a voice whisper in my head.

It stopped me in my tracks. I had never questioned my anxiety; I had always just blindly followed its orders.

I thought about that question briefly before responding silently, "Well, I might faint or get sick, and all these people are here watching me." I could feel the panic rising as I imagined it.

"What will happen if you get off this train right now?" a voice asked me.

"I'll fail my exam and have to retake my entire course even though I'm ready to take the test," I replied, my anxiety turning into frustration.

"Which option is worse?" I asked myself point blank.

I took a deep breath, and the faces around me became clearer. I knew the answer was that fleeing was worse, so I sat down, rebelliously telling myself with the most strength I could muster in the midst of an anxiety storm, "I'm not getting off this train anymore."

Today, that sentiment is still true, in fact probably even more so. I'm a professional speaker, content creator with an online community of over 200,000 thousand people, and I teach professionals and organizations how to use LinkedIn every single day.

Instead of avoiding crowds and the spotlight, I bask in the shared humanity, finding strength and acceptance in the connections that once terrified me. Some days, I think back to that day of my first panic attack and envision my professor. I remember wondering how anybody could be brave enough to clip on a microphone and speak in front of so many people.

Now I am that person. But how?

I want to be clear: this isn't a story about how I kicked anxiety's ass and became a confident networker. I am a regular person, just like you, who was not born with the innate gift of gab or an extroverted personality. Instead, this is about how I learned to navigate and manage my social anxiety and build connections in a way that feels genuine and manageable for me.

Networking is a critical skill to develop in today's age, increasingly so with the rise of AI replacing technical skills. But for some, myself included, it can feel laborious and uncomfortable. Small talk can feel like torture. And let's not forget the ruminating where you replay the same awkward encounter over and over in your mind. Recently, my Uber driver told me to have a great trip and I replied, "You too!" I'm still waking up late at night thinking about it.

When I was approached to write this book, I was determined to create something different than anything else I've ever read. I wanted to write for you, the socially anxious professional who finds networking physically painful sometimes but knows that you need to improve your relationship skills in order to succeed in your career.

This journey of transformation hasn't been easy or straightforward for me, and I'm still learning how to coexist with people in real life again after the pandemic and maternity leave. There were no shortcuts or overnight fixes. I am still me – awkward, shy, and usually sweating during small talk, but thriving in my career in very public spaces despite my social anxiety.

For me, it took a commitment to "not get off the train," a willingness to face my fears head-on, and a lot of trial and error to figure out what felt good (or better) for me when it came to networking.

Throughout this book, I aim to share the strategies that have worked for me, the lessons I've learned along the way, and how you, too, can move from a place of fear and discomfort to a position of strength and confidence in your professional networking.

Remember, the essence of networking is not about being the loudest in the room or always having the right thing to say. We are human, we will all make mistakes – many of them.

It's about making genuine connections, understanding others, and finding common ground in a way that respects both your own boundaries and those of the people you meet. It's about turning what feels like an insurmountable task into an opportunity for growth and learning.

So if you've ever felt like networking is an exclusive club you just can't seem to gain entry to, know that you're not alone.

This book is for anyone who has ever felt out of place, anxious, or simply overwhelmed by the prospect of putting themselves out there. Together, we'll explore how to navigate the networking world in a way that honors our unique challenges and harnesses them into strengths.

Let's embark on this journey together, learning to network without fear, and in doing so, unlocking doors to opportunities we never thought possible. Welcome to *No Fear Networking: A Guide to Building Connections for the Socially Anxious Professional*.

Let's turn the page and begin.

Understanding the Role of Social Anxiety in Networking

1 | Understanding Social Anxiety

The first time that I had stage fright was at a TEDx Ottawa audition in 2017. At the time, I had spoken on a few stages and felt like I had a good handle on my public speaking anxiety.

I wasn't nervous going into it. I had rehearsed my pitch multiple times, and I felt ready. The technician handed me my microphone and wished me good luck. He asked if I had slides.

"No, was I supposed to?" I asked, my heart starting the race.

"Only if you want to," he replied nonchalantly with a disinterested shrug.

"Why didn't I bring slides?" I asked myself. My mind started drifting. *Does everybody else have slides? What if they reject you for not having slides?* My thoughts were scattering rapidly.

I walked out onto the stage. A bright spotlight shone directly into my eyes like high beams on a car.

"Whoa, that's bright," I muttered nervously.

I looked out into the darkened theater. Where were the judges? I could barely make out the outlines of their faces. Were they smiling? Frowning? Pointing and laughing at me for forgetting to create slides?!

I tried to remember my rehearsed lines, but my mind kept shutting off. All I could hear was my heart beating. I felt beads of sweat dripping down my back. The spotlight suddenly felt like a heat lamp.

I felt dizzy. I kept compulsively apologizing. I pulled my notes out of my back pocket and just read off the rest of my pitch before racing off stage.

I ran as fast as I could to my car, leaned into my steering wheel, and cried hard. I knew I had failed.

It was then I realized this was more than just typical nervous "butterflies." This was something pervasive and intense that I later learned had a name: social anxiety disorder.

Understanding Social Anxiety

According to the American Psychiatric Association, social anxiety disorder is "an intense, persistent fear of being watched and judged by others." It is social phobia "characterized by intense anxiety or fear of being judged, negatively evaluated, or rejected in a social or performance situation."[1]

In simpler terms, that means it feels uncomfortable, even scary depending on the severity, to be around other people.

Social anxiety isn't a one-size-fits-all disorder; it's a spectrum from zero to a hundred. Ask most people on the planet if they've ever felt discomfort in social settings and they will answer yes.

Your experience can range from shyness all the way to agoraphobia, the more extreme form of social anxiety that occurs when someone is in a public or crowded place from which a potential escape is difficult, or help may not be readily available.

Some of the symptoms of social anxiety disorder in adults include:

- Avoiding places where other people are present, which could look like eating lunch at your desk instead of the breakroom, avoiding the coffee machine until the area is clear, frequent washroom breaks because the stalls feel safer, or missing social events during and after work with coworkers; perhaps seeking out remote positions that don't require in-person socialization
- Fear of rejection/judgment, feeling self conscious
- Having a hard time making and maintaining eye contact
- Protective body language (crossed arms, standing further away)
- Feeling nauseous and as if your mind is going blank, as if you are experiencing stage fright (This is why many socially anxious people tend to forget names or struggle to pay attention during conversations.)

- Racing heart
- Blushing, sweating, shaking[2]

For the socially anxious professional, myself included, these symptoms don't just happen when you enter a room to network and mingle, but also during these circumstances:

- Being introduced to new people
- Job interviews
- Meetings
- Public speaking in any capacity (boardroom presentations to being on stage)
- Being supervised while performing a task
- Building interpersonal relationships, with coworkers, friends, or romantic partners
- Being on camera or in the spotlight[3]
- Generally, most social encounters that involve other human beings

So not only are the symptoms of social anxiety disorder unpleasant, but they arise during so many situations that occur during everyday life that it's simply not something you can ignore, like I tried to by hibernating in my home.

Social anxiety isn't just about feeling a bit nervous before a big presentation or sensing butterflies in your stomach during a networking event. It digs deeper, casting a shadow over your professional life in ways that can be paralyzing. From the way you perform daily at your job, to your journey up the career ladder, and even how you interact with colleagues, social anxiety touches so many aspects of your professional life.

How Social Anxiety Affects Work Performance

Imagine you're in a meeting, and you've got an idea that you want to share. You look around, and suddenly you start second-guessing yourself. Doubt sets in. You decide to stay silent instead of risking rejection.

Professionals with social anxiety may avoid participating in conversations or meetings, particularly in group settings, because of the fear of being judged. While sometimes this feels like the comfier option in the short term, in the long term it can lead to less visibility and fewer opportunities to contribute.

Now let's say that you did decide to finally speak up and share your idea. But just as you start speaking, your voice cracks a little. Somebody coughs. "Are they coughing or laughing at me?" Your brain wanders. Suddenly, your mind goes blank. You're still speaking, but all of sudden, your articulate idea turns into a jumbled mess. This causes even more anxiety. You wrap up your idea prematurely because all you want to do is flee the room and hide in a corner.

Social anxiety doesn't just limit your ability to speak publicly, but it also hinders your communication. We often think of stage fright as being something that only happens to performers on stage, but truthfully, stage fright can happen during any social interaction!

Maybe you've had your own experience just like this one that is preventing you from seeking out future public speaking opportunities. It's painful – I get it! But there are several ways to reduce both the potential of stage fright and the severity of it, both of which we'll get into shortly.

Social anxiety can also impact your performance at work by inducing procrastination, avoidance, and excessive talking. Social anxiety may contribute to procrastination, particularly due to the fear of negative judgment. A study by Ko and Chang (2019)[4] explored this relationship in college students. The findings indicate that individuals with social anxiety are more likely to have a negative self-perception and engage in behaviors aimed at controlling their self-image because of a fear of failure. Professionals with social anxiety, therefore, may find themselves struggling with tasks that include a real or imagined audience (hello, myself included as I write this book) because of the fear of potential negative feedback.

Avoidance is a coping mechanism used to reduce or escape yucky feelings of anxiety in social settings, where you simply avoid any anxiety-provoking social situations altogether. Although it feels good in the short term (I mean, who doesn't love cocooning in bed after canceling plans to go socialize?), in the long term avoiding things that scare you is harmful because it doesn't help you learn how to live and thrive with social anxiety, only how to placate it.

Earlier, I talked about my first anxiety attack and my experience with agoraphobia. Avoidance was the only coping mechanism that I knew to use at the time. The problem was that avoiding places and things that would potentially cause me anxiety attacks didn't help my anxiety. In fact, the more I avoided leaving my house, the worse my attacks and triggers became, until social anxiety had completely imprisoned me.

Giving in to avoidance behavior also affected my confidence. My self-esteem plummeted because I began to believe the lie that I had no control over my choices.

Once I started to push back on the urges to flee or avoid, I was finally able not only to overcome agoraphobia but also to become a professional speaker, teacher, and creator who spends every day in some sort of social setting.

Doing things that feel initially uncomfortable is like exercising a muscle: the more we look fear in the eyes, the less power it holds. You need a chance to test that crazy worry that your brain has conjured to dispel the feeling that it will come true.

Have you ever watched a horror movie with a blanket covering half your face, but you feel like you have to watch it to the end to be able to go to sleep? Social anxiety is very similar in that we need to stay cozy on the couch until the end of the story so that our brain doesn't create a narrative that doesn't exist.

Beyond testing negative thoughts, participating in social events rather than avoiding them gives space for new positive experiences.

If you had told me years ago on that train that someday I would become a public speaker, I would have never believed you, but I also never would have guessed that I would feel so exhilarated by teaching people something new! After years of trying different roles and climbing the ladder, I've finally found something that I truly love doing, but I would never have discovered that if I hadn't gone outside my comfort zone to begin with. Maybe you don't want to become a public speaker, but you may find that attending more social events could lead to new friendships, opportunities, and skills that you never imagined possible!

However, stepping out of your comfort zone can sometimes lead to unexpected behaviors. One of these behaviors, oddly enough, is also related to social anxiety: excessive talking. Or, as I like to call it when I'm in this mode, word vomiting all over the place.

Let's imagine that you decide you're going to go for it. Instead of reorganizing your sock drawer, you're going to put on your best pair of polyester pants and head out to a local meetup one night.

The moment you step into the overcrowded room, your anxiety spikes. Everybody seems to know each other, laughing like old friends. You finally work up the courage to join a circle of chatting colleagues, and suddenly an uncontrollable monolog spills out of you.

You begin with your name…then you start rambling about the charcuterie board…then you spiral into tangents on everything from the weather forecast and global warming to your dog's predisposition to UTIs.

When you finally pause to breathe, you notice a mix of polite smiles and body language that screams, "Get me away from this conversation." Your heart sinks as the realization hits: your nervous monolog might have just torpedoed your first impression.

It seems absolutely bonkers that one coping mechanism for social anxiety is avoiding certain situations while another is overtalking or rambling, but nervousness can lead to people to try and overcompensate. Sometimes, what looks like a confident extrovert is actually somebody trying to "fake it till they make it" and quiet the voices swirling around in their mind by talking over them.

This shows up often for me, particularly in situations where the person I'm speaking to isn't talkative. I feel like I'm subconsciously trying to feed them talking triggers to avoid the dreaded silence and shoe stare that sometimes happens during networking conversations. I also do this when I feel intimidated by the person I'm speaking to and I want them to feel like I'm useful or helpful. The worst part of overtalking is the inevitable rumination that comes afterwards where you smack your forehead and wonder why on earth you couldn't stop talking about your acid reflux (true story).

The moral of the story here is that social anxiety doesn't just mean avoidance; it can manifest in so many different, unexpected ways.

How Social Anxiety Affects Career Advancement

Social anxiety doesn't affect only your everyday performance in social situations at work. In the long term, it can also affect your career success and potential for promotions. One of the reasons for this is because, at a cellular level, social anxiety reflects a fear of inadequacy. Deep down, you feel like you don't measure up somehow and people are going to judge you when they realize that you're unworthy.

One of the ways social anxiety manifests, therefore, is through people-pleasing. You overcompensate for those feelings of inadequacy by saying yes to people and projects that you shouldn't because you don't want to let anyone down.

At every place I worked, one of my ongoing issues was overpromising and then burning out. I was the employee you could call on a Sunday because I'd rather work on call and unpaid than ever dare assert myself and set up boundaries.

The problem is that saying yes to one thing means saying no to something else. Saying yes to working for free on a Sunday, for example, meant less time to spend on the hobbies that fulfilled me and on crucial family time. It meant that by the time I "returned" to work on a Monday, I was already tired. I spent much of my workweek exhaustingly trying to please everybody until I would inevitably burn out and have to take time off or move on to a new role.

The other issue with people-pleasing is that if you always say yes, you never learn the art of assertiveness. On top of not learning how to say no, you also miss out on opportunities to learn how to ask for what you really want, like that promotion you deserve. Assertiveness is a critical skill to be able to make your career dreams a reality.

Another way that social anxiety affects career advancement is by impacting performance during high-pressure social situations, like my TEDx audition. There are so many situations where you have to show up with confidence to get what you want, such as during team meetings, one-on-one closed-door meetings with your boss, and job interviews. Social anxiety can make you crumble in those scenarios.

And finally, social anxiety can affect career advancement because of avoidance of social situations. From one overcaffeinated socially anxious professional to another: relationships matter.

Rising to the Challenge

If you want to get what you want — that big promotion, a new role at an incredible company, awesome new clients — you are going to need to build relationships. People buy from people they vibe with. As much as we like to believe that we are perfectly logical, rational beings, we make decisions based on emotions. So, I'm going to be real with you: you need to learn how to deal with people. Some folks are born with the ability to network easily; we are not those people, but we have to work with the cards we've been dealt.

And now that we've explored social anxiety in a nutshell and all the ways it might manifest as a professional, let's jump into the good stuff.

Diving deep into the world of social anxiety and its grip on our professional lives can feel heavy and impossible to navigate. I know that just writing about some of my experiences with social anxiety triggered my own fight-or-flight response even years later!

Yet, as challenging as it can feel to try and thrive with an anxious heart, I also see a huge opportunity here to explore the possibilities and strategies to develop true connections in our work lives. Every challenge, every moment of discomfort, is also an invitation to step up, lean into the fear, and grow stronger from it.

As we pivot to the next part of our adventure, keep in mind that the goal isn't to silence the anxious whispers but to learn how to coexist with them. So grab your favorite mug, pour yourself a warm cup of java, and let's dive into mastering no fear networking.

2 | The Power of Networking

Let's face it, the idea of networking can conjure up images of forced smiles, uncomfortable silences, and the pressure to make the right first impression.

For a long time, for me, it felt just like stepping back in time to high school, scanning the cafeteria to try and find a familiar face and have a seat. I wasn't a popular kid in high school and struggled to find a group that I truly fit into, and that feeling continued well into my university days.

It wasn't until the day that I overcame agoraphobia that something finally clicked for me. As I stood there, rocking gently on the train in an attempt to soothe my frayed nerves, bracing myself for the mockery I feared would come, an unexpected scene unfolded instead.

A woman casually retrieved a mirror from her purse, inspecting her teeth for any stray remnants of her last meal. Nearby, a teenage boy sneakily sniffed under his arm for body odor before confidently draping an arm around his companion.

That's when it hit me: other people aren't as daunting as I had imagined. We're all navigating our own insecurities, each of us simply trying to find our way.

The moment of realization that shifted my entire approach to networking wasn't about strategy, tactics, or making flawless first impressions. It was about understanding that, at its core, networking is interacting with other human beings who are navigating their own imperfections and insecurities.

The "why behind the hi" became clear.

Networking wasn't a stage performance where I played a part; it was an opportunity for growth, connection, and support. This shift in understanding laid the groundwork for the benefits that networking has brought into my life since then that eventually lead me to a career that I love and opportunities that I could never have imagined, which I'd like to share with you. Let's get into it.

Networking Unlocks Possibilities

When you engage in networking, it's not just about exchanging business cards or collecting new LinkedIn connections like you're gathering trophies for a display case. Sure, some might play it as a transactional game, eyeing each interaction for what they can extract. To borrow a phrase from the *Bachelor* franchise, they're not in it for the "right reasons," and by doing so, they overlook the essence and transformative potential of networking.

That hollow, transactional feel? You recognize it when it happens. It feels icky, disconnected from the more meaningful engagements that true networking brings.

But when networking is authentic, when it's driven by a genuine desire for collaboration and connection, that's when the magic unfolds.

For instance, consider the situation of a friend asking you to recommend a real estate agent to help sell their home. When you think of the perfect person for the job, there's a spark, an enthusiasm in your recommendation. Why? Because you're not just passing along a name; you're sharing trust. You've built a relationship with this person that extends beyond the surface; you genuinely like and respect them. There's a joy in supporting those with whom you have positive relationships.

A couple of years back, I found myself gearing up to speak at a major content marketing conference in Cleveland. The networking area was massive, decked out with sleek high-top tables and napkins covered with logos. The sheer scale of it sent my anxiety skyrocketing and my heart pounding.

"I'll give it 30 minutes, then head back to the hotel," I whispered to myself.

Leaning against the bar, nervously awaiting my much-needed glass of wine, I bumped into Viveka, a fellow speaker I'd crossed paths with a few times before. Viveka's presence was like a breath of fresh air; her warmth and authenticity always made these networking gigs feel less like work and more like catching up with an old buddy.

There we were, two LinkedIn nerds, theoretically in competition, but it never really felt that way. Our bond was solidified not just by our session content overlap but by a shared sarcastic sense of humor and, more recently, the painful experience of losing parents suddenly.

As our conversation flowed effortlessly from LinkedIn strategies to personal ambitions, I shared my dream for the year: "I'm really hoping to become a LinkedIn Learning Instructor and create my own course."

Viveka's eyes widened. "Michaela!" she burst out. "Did you know I'm one of their instructors? Let me introduce you to my contact there!"

Her enthusiasm was infectious, and I was excited, but internally, I was skeptical anything would come of it. Yet later that night, as I flopped onto my hotel bed and scrolled through my phone, I found Viveka had already connected me with her LinkedIn Learning contact via email. I was astounded.

The whirlwind didn't stop there. By the next morning, as I sat on the plane waiting for takeoff, her contact had gotten in touch, eager to see a proposal from me.

And just like that, a casual chat over wine transformed into a pivotal career opportunity. That night in Cleveland wasn't just another networking event; it was a reminder that sometimes the most impactful connections come from simply sharing a drink and opening up.

Networking Gets You the Inside Scoop

Imagine you're wandering the busy streets of New York City's East Village. On a seemingly ordinary quest for a bite to eat, you find yourself stepping into a hot dog joint, ready to devour a locally famous frankfurter, ideally slathered in yellow mustard.

But you aren't here just for a late-night snack. You've heard rumors of a hidden gem tucked away within these walls, a speakeasy where conversations are shared over craft cocktails. You spot the vintage phone booth and dial the secret number as your excitement builds, a thrill sparked by the anticipation of an adventure that's waiting for you on the other side.

The back wall of the phone booth swings open, and clink of glasses and murmured conversations fill the air. The Please Don't Tell cocktail bar welcomes you with its warm, dimly lit ambiance. But PDT is more than just a bar; it's a reminder that some of the most extraordinary experiences await just beyond a hidden door, accessible to those willing to look for them.

Networking, much like the PDT speakeasy adventure, is a gateway to the hidden opportunities and insights that exist just beyond the surface, accessible through networking. It all starts with a hello, a candid conversation, and the courage to reach out and connect.

In short, networking is your backstage pass to the inner workings of your industry or field, granting you access to insights, wisdom, and opportunities that are not visible without the willingness to get uncomfortable and network.

So, take that step and discover what lies beyond the telephone booth of networking. The journey might just transform your career in ways you never imagined.

Networking Elevates Your Gabbing Game

It's time for some real talk: let's drop the "I'm not cut out for networking" act.

Trust me, I've been in those shoes, convinced I was too awkward, too much of a weirdo, too anxious to mingle in social settings. I convinced myself to become a hermit, dodging any form of social interaction.

So how did I go from that to somebody who speaks with thousands of people daily for a living? I didn't put on a pantsuit version of Cinderella's glass slipper and magically transform into a networking princess.

What changed, then? My mindset.

I had to rewrite the narrative I'd spun around my identity and capabilities. And yes, picking up this new skill was uncomfortable, even downright terrifying at times.

And guess what? Sometimes it still is.

But there's a newfound grace and confidence in understanding that I don't need to morph into someone else. Instead, I simply need to treat networking like any other skill.

One unexpected benefit that I've discovered through networking is that practicing social interactions doesn't just help you in a professional sense, but across all areas of life as well. Networking introduces you to all sorts of people and stories, which in turn can make you more empathetic and informed about the world around you. It introduces you to a rainbow of viewpoints and experiences, which encourages you to consider different perspectives.

Networking also improves your listening skills. One of the biggest challenges for me in the beginning (and still to this day) is listening to understand, not just to respond. When you're not fully engaged in listening, conversations can quickly become disjointed. You find yourself scrambling for words or giving responses that don't quite match the tone of the conversation because you missed the essence of what was being shared. Active listening isn't innate; it's a skill refined over time through intentional practice, but the benefits are not just becoming a better networker, but also a better friend, parent, and/or partner.

Networking also improves your nonverbal communication. Being a socially anxious public speaker is not always an easy gig. Often, because of my role, people assume that I am extroverted and a confident networker. Spoiler alert: I am not, and many "performers" are socially anxious. We'll chat more about that in a bit.

However, because of this assumption, I've run into a few situations where the person got angry at me for being snobby and standoffish. When I started networking more often, I could "fake" my interactions verbally, but not nonverbally. I would slink away, frown, cross my arms, turn my body. I didn't even realize that I was doing it, but the person I was interacting with sometimes did. Once, I had somebody send me a message after an event saying how disappointed they were to finally meet in person and have me be so standoffish (to put it kindly).

I won't lie; it felt like a gut punch. That message, that single piece of feedback, was like a mirror suddenly held up to my world. It didn't just reflect back my awkwardness or social anxiety; it reflected the gap between how I wanted to connect with people and the reality of how I was perceived.

This was another pivotal moment for me in my journey to becoming the type of networker that I wanted to be.

Instead of throwing on a blazer and playing a role both on and off stage, I often start with a bit of a disclaimer that these events are a challenge for me, and making that confession feels like a sense of relief shared between me and the person in front of me, who is usually struggling with the same fears.

Personally, I couldn't change my nonverbal communication without letting go of the mask I thought I needed to succeed. I stopped trying to play a role and started to lean into being myself. The shift was everything for me. My body language naturally became more open and inviting as I became more comfortable in my own skin.

Smiles came easier, my stance was relaxed, and eye contact didn't feel as torturous.

This transformation didn't erase my social anxiety overnight, and if we met today, I'd probably still need to change my deodorant afterward, but it significantly bridged the gap between how I felt and how I was perceived, and that's a huge win in my books.

Networking Grows Your Support Circle

The single most important lesson I've learned throughout my career is this: success is never a solo journey.

When I first mentioned I was writing this book, a common reaction was, "I'd love to network more, but I just can't stand people." This confession often came with a laugh, but behind that humor is a grain of truth that many of us can relate to.

Navigating the social waters of adulthood, particularly within a networking context, can indeed feel scary. It's even more challenging when you're grappling with social anxiety or have been scarred by past interactions that left you feeling used.

But here's a thought: perhaps it's not people we hate, but those awkward, forced, or superficial interactions that leave us feeling disconnected and misunderstood.

I remember once, shortly after having my baby, I reached out via Instagram to another mom I'd met in a Mommy and Me swim class. We'd hit it off and found ourselves diving into deep conversations on various topics. One day, feeling overwhelmed, I confessed to her, "The newborn phase is killing me. The sleepless nights, the constant crying…I just don't know how people handle it."

Her response was well-intentioned but missed the mark for me: "But you're going to miss this time with her."

While she wasn't wrong that I might look back fondly on those early days with my daughter, the response made me feel isolated in my struggle, steeped in shame rather than supported or seen.

It's these moments of disconnect that often fuel our aversion to social interactions, mistakenly interpreted as a dislike for people. It felt as though my anxious mind was on standby, seizing any evidence to justify my inclination toward hermit life. It took me a few days to process that interaction fully.

While chatting with my mom about the conversation, she stopped me and asked, "Mick, would you be friends with this person if you didn't have kids the same age, or is that the only thing you have in common?"

That hit me hard.

I realized that in my quest for finding my support circle in those days of messy early motherhood, I was skipping the most important step: seeking genuine connections over convenient ones.

Feeling inspired, I messaged a different friend who also had a young daughter. Our bond had strengthened over our shared love for thrifting baby clothes, a hobby that brought me so much joy amidst the sleep-deprived haze.

"Do you think there are other moms who enjoy thrifting too? Maybe we should start a group chat?" I hesitated before sending, unsure of her response.

The next day, I sent a private message to another friend, who also had a daughter close in age and to whom I had been talking about the joy of thrifting baby clothes, even in the midst of our zombie-like state of sleep deprivation. I nervously asked her,

"Hey, do you think there are other moms like us who enjoy thrifting too? Maybe we should start a little group chat?"

Her enthusiastic reply came swiftly: "Absolutely! My friend would love that."

And so, a little over a year ago, our group chat was born. Initially small, it has blossomed into a vibrant community of over 20 moms from across North America. Our discussions may have started with thrifting baby clothes, but they've evolved into so much more. We've created a unique support network where moms can openly share about everything from postpartum depression and anxiety to celebrating the latest sale find.

The chat has transformed into our own digital sanctuary, much like cozying up on a friend's sofa, wine glass in hand. It stands as proof that genuine bonds can flourish even in digital realms, challenging the notion that social media is the nemesis of real-world interaction. We'll dive deeper into this later, but for now, it's clear: authentic connections can and do thrive online, but you must be willing to face the discomfort of finding your people.

When networking is done with genuine intentions, the benefits are truly limitless. A community can lift you up, push you forward, and stand with you through thick and thin.

One of the reasons why I decided to start my networking journey is that I wanted to find people who appreciated me for *me*, not transactional, conditional relationships that only exist as long as you are in a certain position or working at a certain company.

Let's have another real chat, shall we? You deserve more.

You deserve more than spending every workday wrapped in doubts, questioning your worth, and fretting over the stability of your future. It's exhausting and unnerving, living in the shadow of "what ifs" and the fear of the unknown.

What if the thing you've been avoiding (networking) is just what you need? It brings to mind that classic Rolling Stones tune "You Can't Always Get What You Want," which echoes a timeless truth:

> "You can't always get what you want/But if you try sometime you'll find/You get what you need."[1]

Networking can often feel like an overwhelming task, but it is in fact the bridge to a world where your worth is recognized, your potential is untapped, and your future is bright with possibilities. It's about finding your sanctuary in the professional jungle – a group of people who understand your struggles, celebrate your successes, and offer a hand when you stumble. Networking isn't being trapped in a room (okay, we know that's debatable); it can be the most liberating thing you can do, as it has been for me.

So, to anyone who feels hesitant about networking, fearing it's a realm of superficial exchanges and awkward small talk, think back to every cool experience you've had in life. Where did it begin? Maybe it was deciding to attend that job interview or chatting with an old coworker over coffee. Maybe it was as small as accepting the LinkedIn request from somebody you hadn't met.

No matter what your specific story is, it likely started with a simple act of reaching out, a moment of bravery on an otherwise ordinary day. Each of these actions is a form of networking, a step toward something bigger, even if it didn't seem like it at the time.

Networking isn't just about schmoozing, at least not the way we're going to tackle it together in this book; it's about building bridges to new adventures, learning opportunities, and, yes, sometimes even friendships where we talk about Spanx and soothers.

So, let's reframe the way we talk about networking. Instead of thinking of it as just a painful task, let's remember that it could be the start of something awesome. It's the story of how a casual conversation can lead to your next adventure. It's proof that the universe rewards those willing to step outside their comfort zone and say, "Hello, I'm here. I'm shaky and feel like I want to beeline for the nearest washroom, but I'm here."

Networking isn't just a tool for advancement; it's a journey to, as the very wise men of the Rolling Stones once sang, "You get what you need."

Thriving in the Professional World as a Social Wallflower

By now, you've got the memo: networking is a big deal.

Chances are, you were onto this long before you turned the first page of this book. But let's address the elephant in the room – social anxiety, aka the reason that the thought of stepping into a bustling room full of strangers can feel daunting, if not outright terrifying.

Don't worry, we're going to dive deep into strategies for navigating social anxiety and making networking feel like a breeze in the chapters ahead. But remember, networking isn't just about extending your hand to others; it's equally about reaching inward to discover the gifts you carry within.

What if I told you that the very thing making networking seem like an uphill battle could also be your hidden superpower? Yes, your social anxiety, which often feels like a massive roadblock, might just be the unique edge you need to flourish in networking environments.

Clinical psychologist Dr. Ellen Henriksen, author of *How to Be Yourself: Quiet Your Inner Critic and Rise Above Social Anxiety*, explains why she loves working with those with social anxiety:

> "Social anxiety is a package deal, and it often comes bundled with strengths like high standards and empathy and being helpful and altruistic. People who have social anxiety are often good listeners and conscientious and they work hard to get along with fellow humans. And those are all really amazing strengths that won't go away even as people work on their social anxiety."[2]

That's why this book isn't about magically erasing your social anxiety as if it were an inconvenient blemish. It's about navigating through it, understanding its contours, and learning strategies to handle it.

The very sensations that send a shiver down my spine and set my heart racing also turn me into a master of reading the room. I've honed an acute sense of when someone's not quite sincere by the twinkle in their eye, or when someone in the room feels overlooked, betrayed by their nervous interaction with a coffee mug. I'm instinctively drawn to bring them back into the fold.

We, the socially anxious, are paradoxically the ones you can rely on for unwavering support. We're the guardians of inclusivity, always striving to ensure everyone feels acknowledged and seen, despite our own urge to vanish into the background.

In two studies, 260 participants, some with social anxiety and others with social anxiety disorder, were shown videos of people talking about times they felt excluded in high school.[3] Participants then guessed how these people felt, and these guesses were compared to how the people in the videos said they felt. This comparison helped researchers see how accurately participants could understand others' emotions.

Not surprisingly, the results showed that both groups with anxiety were better at picking up on others' emotions than people without anxiety, even when it came to stories of being left out. This ability didn't change much in different situations, showing that it's a consistent trait for those across the spectrum of social anxiety.

So, remember: your journey with social anxiety in the networking world is not about shedding part of yourself; it's about embracing and amplifying the kickass qualities you bring to the high-top table. Let's discover how to make your mark, not despite your social anxiety, but because of it.

Quiet Giants: Success Stories of the Socially Anxious

Imagine the person you watch on the big screen, whose music blasts through your headphones, or whose quotes are hung on posters around your office space as inspiration, pausing backstage, taking a deep breath, and battling the same butterflies in their stomach that you might feel before a big meeting or a social event.

One of the biggest misconceptions about social anxiety is that it only affects those who are naturally introverted or shy, that we'll "know them when we see them," and that people in the limelight are immune to feeling it.

Many of the same people who grace magazine covers and sell out arenas also deal with the clammy hands, racing hearts, and sometimes overwhelming urge to run away and hide that come with social anxiety. In fact, as we'll see in later chapters, sometimes being in the public eye is a coping mechanism used to avoid situations where social roles are not as defined.

For now, let's take a look at some of the famous faces who have spoken openly about their challenges of being in the spotlight with social anxiety and how they've learned to manage it and thrive socially.

Emma Stone, multiple Academy Award winner, and one of Hollywood's most beloved actresses, has struggled with anxiety since she was a little girl. In an interview, she recalled:

> "From eight to 10, I was borderline agoraphobic....I couldn't go to friends' houses, I had deep separation anxiety with my mom....I was so paranoid about everything....We truly thought I wasn't going to be able to move out of the house and move away ever. How would I go to college? How would I do any of this if I couldn't be at a friend's house for five minutes?"[4]

Stone credits therapy, meditation, and reaching out to talk to people for overcoming her crippling social anxiety. She also shares the importance of pushing yourself outside of your comfort zone and owning your story. "[It's] healing to just talk about it and own it and realize that this is something that is part of me, but it is not who I am." As for whether she thinks people with social anxiety have the ability to succeed, she says, "you can still get out there and achieve dreams and form really great relationships and connections."

Barbra Streisand is an iconic American singer, actress, and filmmaker whose battle with social anxiety may surprise you. In her memoir, *My Name Is Barbra*, she explains that her stage fright after forgetting her lines at a big live concert was so great that she avoided public performances for nearly 30 years.

In an interview with Diane Sawyer, Streisand recalls, "I didn't sing and charge people for 27 years because of that night. ... I was like, 'God, I don't know. What if I forget the words again?'"[5] Barbra finally returned to the stage in the 1990s and credits both a teleprompter and medication for helping with her anxiety before performances.

Naomi Osaka is one of the most iconic figures in tennis. She has won multiple Grand Slam titles, including the US Open and the Australian Open. She's known for her powerful serve, but would you have guessed that she also struggles with social anxiety?

She took to social media in 2021 to share her battle as she announced that she was dropping out of the French Open: "Anyone that knows me knows I'm introverted, and anyone that has seen me at tournaments will notice that I'm often wearing headphones as that helps dull my social anxiety."[6]

She went on to share her difficulties with dealing with the press. "I'm not a natural public speaker and I get huge waves of anxiety when I speak to the world's media. I get really nervous and find it stressful to always try to engage and give you the best answers I can."

Since then, Osaka has said that she's received an outpouring of support, started seeing a therapist regularly, and launched a partnership with Modern Health, an app to connect people with mental health resources. When she returned to the court after taking a break, she said in an interview,

▌ "I really had a blast on court for the first time in a while,"[7]

Shonda Rimes, a prolific American television producer and screenwriter, went on a yearlong journey to take charge of her social anxiety. In her book *Year of Yes: How to Dance It Out, Stand in the Sun, and Be Your Own Person*, she chronicles how she decided to go from avoidance to achievement by vowing to say "yes" to the things that scared her for a year.

Her raw, real advice? "Be brave. Be amazing. Be worthy. And every single time you get the chance? Stand up in front of people. Let them see you. Speak. Be heard. Go ahead and have the dry mouth. Let your heart beat so, so fast. Watch everything move in slow motion. So what. You what? You pass out, you die, you poop? No. (And this is really the only lesson you'll ever need to know.)"[8]

One person that you probably didn't expect to see included here is Warren Buffet, investor, philanthropist, and one of the most successful businessmen of all time. But Buffet struggled with public speaking early on in his career.

> "I was so terrified that I just couldn't speak in public," he details in his biography, *The Snowball: Warren Buffett and the Business of Life.* "I would throw up. In fact, I arranged my life so that I never had to get up in front of anybody."[9]

To overcome his fear, he took a Dale Carnegie course on public speaking, where he learned how to speak in groups through uncomfortable repetition. "Some of it is…just doing it and practicing," Buffett shared.

Perhaps most surprising of all, Mahatma Gandhi, Indian leader of nonviolence and justice, also battled social anxiety. In his book, *My Experiments with Truth*, Gandhi describes his experiences, some of which might hit close to home (they certainly do for me!):

> "I was elected to the Executive Committee of the Vegetarian Society… but I always felt tongue-tied. I sat quite silent. Not that I never felt tempted to speak. But I was at a loss to know how to express myself."[10]

He also seemed to battle imposter syndrome, a condition in which someone doubts their abilities and feels like a fraud and a common component of social anxiety. In his book, he writes, "All the rest of the members appeared to me to be better informed than I."

Even though Gandhi was able to speak more as he gained practice, he also credited it as an advantage:

> "My hesitancy in speech, which was once an annoyance, is now a pleasure. Its greatest benefit has been that it has taught me the economy of words. I have naturally formed the habit of restraining my thoughts…a man of few words will rarely be thoughtless in his speech; he will measure every word…shyness has been in reality my shield and buckler. It has allowed me to grow. It has helped me in my discernment of truth."

Whoa. Gandhi's wisdom here is a game changer.

Our quiet moments and the times we choose our words carefully aren't just about being shy; they're our superpowers.

They help us grow, uncover our truths, and communicate with purpose. As we've seen through the stories of various public figures, social anxiety doesn't limit what we're capable of achieving. The moral of the story from celebs to CEOs? Dive into what terrifies you.

If the thought of networking still makes you uneasy, hang tight. The upcoming chapter is a mindset makeover designed to equip and inspire you to head into your next event with confidence and a new perspective. Let's get prepping!

PART

II

Prepping for Success

3 | Mindset Makeover for People Who Can't People

Think about the last time you turned down an invitation because the thought of small talk made your stomach churn, or the moment you stayed silent in a meeting, even though you had something important to add.

Social anxiety doesn't just keep you from stepping into the limelight, it holds you back from forming meaningful connections, discovering new opportunities, and embracing the personal growth that is rightfully yours.

In this chapter, we'll create a plan that pushes you but feels doable. Every small win is a reason to celebrate, and with each step, you'll be building the confidence you need not just to get by in social situations but to own the room. Ready to dive in? Let's do this!

Overcoming Social Fear

To overcome social fear, you need to realize first what *not* overcoming it is costing you.

Imagine all those golden opportunities for growth and connection just beyond your grasp, along with brilliant ideas that could change the course of your career, all fading away because of that nagging feeling of dread. It's about the moments of hesitation, the "what ifs" that prevent you from entering a room, sharing your thoughts in a meeting, or saying yes to an invitation that could lead somewhere amazing. Let's explore stories from people who've faced these challenges, showing you the true cost of allowing social anxiety to decide your fate.

Jamie's Story: A Missed Promotion in Digital Marketing

Jamie had always seen herself as a contender for the next big leap in her digital marketing career. Her dedication was obvious, her campaigns not just meeting but surpassing benchmarks set by her team.

She knew she had the chops for the promotion that was up for grabs. The only obstacle? A presentation to the senior management, a perfect platform to demonstrate her awesomeness. But as the date drew near, Jamie's social anxiety, a silent shadow that had accompanied her throughout her career, loomed larger than ever.

The thought of standing before the company's decision-makers, with every eye on her, was paralyzing. So, when Alex, a colleague of Jamie's with a more outward confidence, mentioned his interest in leading the presentation, Jamie felt an initial sense of relief wash over her. "Maybe it's for the best," she reasoned, trying to silence the nagging voice that told her she was making a mistake.

Alex took the stage, and Jamie watched from the sidelines as her work, her ideas, were met with nods of approval. The presentation was a success, catapulting Alex into the role Jamie had silently yearned for.

Elena's Story: The Dream Job That Slipped Away

Elena had always dreamed of working for a certain tech startup, renowned for its innovative culture and happy employees. An annual tech conference, known for connecting talented professionals with industry leaders, was happening in her city.

Elena knew this was her golden ticket. But as the event approached, the thought of navigating a sea of unknown faces and striking up conversations made her stomach churn. She convinced herself she wasn't ready, telling herself, "Next year, I'll go."

Weeks later, Elena learned while scrolling on LinkedIn that the startup had been scouting for talent at that very conference, offering on-the-spot interviews to attendees. A friend who braved the event landed a dream job, thanks to a casual chat by the coffee stand.

The realization hit Elena hard: her social anxiety had cost her not just an opportunity but a chance at her dream.

Recognize What You're Missing Out on Because of Social Anxiety

As you reflect on Jamie's and Elena's stories, consider the negative impact social anxiety has had on your own life. What opportunities have you missed due to social anxiety? Have there been moments when you've stood on the sidelines, watching as others took the stage that was meant for you? How about the times you've let the chance to connect with someone slip through your fingers because the fear of reaching out was too scary?

Take a moment to reflect on these questions and consider writing down your thoughts:

- What specific opportunities have I missed because of social anxiety?
- How has social anxiety affected my personal growth and career advancement?
- What dreams have I put on hold because of my fear of social situations?

By acknowledging these moments, you begin the journey toward overcoming your social anxiety. Remember, recognizing the cost is the initial step toward mustering the courage for change.

Identifying Safety Behaviors

According to the American Psychological Association "Dictionary of Psychology," safety behaviors are "a behavior performed by an anxious individual in an attempt to minimize or prevent a feared catastrophe."[1]

In other words, it's the things that you do to make you feel safe in situations that feel not-so-safe. For example, I tend to disappear to the washroom often during networking events to try and catch my breath, I struggle to hold and keep eye contact because I'm afraid of seeming creepy, and I name-drop and mention accomplishments in settings in which I feel undeserving to talk to the people involved.

Here are some other examples of safety behaviors of socially anxious professionals:

- Rehearsing conversations
- Scrolling on your phone
- Only talking to people who you already know
- Avoiding social situations or canceling plans to socialize
- Heading straight to the bar
- Mentally planning escape routes
- Fidgeting or self-soothing
- Giving one-word answers to avoid rejections[2]

Dr. Ellen Henriksen calls safety behaviors "the life preserver that holds you underwater,"[3] because although they may help to reduce symptoms of social anxiety temporarily, in the long term they are actually counterproductive. While they are intended to provide relief, they ultimately keep you submerged in a state of anxiety, preventing you from learning to swim in social waters on your own.

At this point, you might be thinking, "Ummm, Mick, I'm quite comfortable in the shallow end over here, thank you very much."

I get it. Safety behaviors have likely been a part of you for a very long time, and they feel cozy in their familiarity. It's like wrapping yourself in a warm blanket on a cold day. These behaviors have been your go-to, your safety net in social situations that feel overwhelming. But here's the thing – staying in the shallow end, while comfortable, also means you're missing out on the adventure that lies in the deeper waters.

The true downside to safety behaviors is that every time you use one, you're reinforcing the belief that you can't handle the deep end on your own. But what if you can?

We believe what we experience. So if you are continually avoiding social situations and choosing to watch Netflix in bed instead, you're missing out on the opportunity to disprove and challenge your social fears.

Let's take a personal example to illustrate this point. One of my safety behaviors I find most annoying is my tendency to shift into bragging mode. This usually happens when I'm interacting with someone highly accomplished or whom I greatly admire.

It's not that I believe I'm better than the other person; rather, I find myself name-dropping, casually mentioning my achievements, and essentially trying to elevate my own social "value." It feels almost like an automatic response, one that I sometimes find so hard to control.

However, the aftermath of such interactions leaves me feeling anything but proud. Instead of feeling satisfied with myself and the conversation, I'm immediately filled with dread and shame for resorting to such tactics.

Why? Because it feels as though I've had the entire exchange behind a mask. I don't feel like I'm being genuine; to me it reeks of low self-esteem, and even if I've been chatting with somebody for an hour, I feel like they just walked away not knowing me at all.

Similarly, other safety behaviors that I've used in the past – like fidgeting, giving one-word answers, and mentally planning escape routes – all give the impression to the person that I'm speaking to that I'm totally uninterested in the conversation, which is the opposite of my intentions when networking.

Dr. Henriksen agrees: "While safety behaviors serve to reduce one's anxiety, they can send an unintentionally unfriendly message. Wearing sunglasses and earbuds sends the message 'Don't talk to me.' Peppering a conversation partner with questions leaves them feeling interrogated. Not revealing anything about your life makes others have to work hard to get to know you. Safety behaviors make individuals with social anxiety appear snobby, aloof, or distant, when really they are just anxious."

Think about yourself again, what are some of your own safety behaviors? What sort of impression do you think they're giving to the person you're speaking to?

Actively participating in situations while consciously reducing safety behaviors is critical for you to grow into a no fear networker as it sends a signal to your brain that you are indeed safe without relying on these behavioral crutches.

For example, let's say I engage in a conversation with someone I deeply admire and make a true effort not to resort to bragging mode. In doing so, a significant shift can occur within me. By engaging in that interaction on a purely human level, without feeling the need to drop names or boast, I disrupt the narrative that acceptance hinges on showcasing my accomplishments. I am telling myself that I am enough as I am.

Whoa, how powerful is that?!

To truly overcome social fear, you need to be willing to drop the extra stuff that's weighing you down. While it's hard to let go of the things that feel comfortable, it's time to tell yourself better stories about your ability and worth.

Identifying Triggers

Meeting new people, making small talk, presenting to a group, being on Zoom calls – social anxiety can pop up for people during a wide variety of social situations. Some people feel it during any and all social situations; others feel it only under specific circumstances. Knowing what fans the flames of your social anxiety is an important step to learning how to manage it when it strikes.

According to Anxiety Canada, most social anxiety triggers in adults fall into two categories: performance situations and interpersonal interactions.[4]

Performance situations are "where people feel they are being observed by others," such as:

- Participating in meetings
- Going on job interviews
- Attending formal networking events
- Giving or receiving a performance review
- Posting on social media
- Presenting a proposal
- Leading group activities
- Eating in front of others
- Hosting a Zoom call

Even things like making a phone call or writing an email can trigger social anxiety (I can attest to this one!) because of the fear of rejection or judgment.

Interpersonal interactions are "situations where people are interacting with others and developing closer relationships," such as:

- Meeting new people
- Chatting with coworkers
- Attending support groups

- Attending therapy (both group and individual because of the fear of judgment)
- Participating in social functions at work
- Inviting others to do things
- Participating in hobby groups

Now why might it be important to know that your triggers are, for instance, eating in front of others and formal networking events? First, it allows you to anticipate and prepare. By knowing what situations are likely to trigger your social anxiety, you can develop coping strategies in advance to help manage your anxiety when it arises.

Identifying triggers helps you to differentiate between situations where you may feel more comfortable and those where you may need extra support or assistance. For example, consider these two scenarios:

Mark is a recent graduate who is eager to find a job quickly so that he can afford more than ramen noodles and Rice Krispies. He knows that formal networking events are one of his triggers for social anxiety, but he feels pressured to get out there and meet people. When he receives an invitation to a prestigious networking event hosted by his local chamber of commerce, Mark feels his stomach churn when he sees that it's followed by a sit-down dinner. He reluctantly RSVPs yes.

As he arrives at the event venue, he is greeted by a sea of unfamiliar faces and a palpable sense of pressure to make a good impression.

As people flow into the room wearing suit jackets and cocktail dresses, John's anxiety mounts. He struggles to engage in small talk and approach potential contacts. He finds himself retreating to the sidelines, avoiding eye contact, and second-guessing his every word.

Sweating and dizzy, Mark finds the nearest exit and bolts into a nearby cab. "I hate networking," he mumbles to himself. "This is why I never should have tried."

Now, alternatively, imagine this scenario:

Mark, still jobless and needing to find a new position before next month's rent is due, decides to give networking one last shot. This time, though, he decides to take a different approach.

Instead of attending another formal networking event with a sit-down dinner, he opts for a more casual gathering at a local coffee shop. He invites a few friends from his college days who work in the same industry and understand his struggles with social anxiety. As he arrives at the coffee shop, he is greeted by familiar faces and a warm, inviting atmosphere.

Instead of feeling overwhelmed by the pressure to make a good impression, Mark feels supported and understood by his friends. They engage in meaningful conversations, share job search tips, and offer words of encouragement. Mark finds himself gradually opening up, sharing his experiences and goals with others. Heck, Mark even drank a mocha latte and nibbled on a croissant sandwich during the conversation!

By choosing a setting that feels more comfortable and familiar, Mark can navigate his social anxiety more easily. He leaves the gathering feeling excited and motivated to continue his job search, knowing that he has the support of friends who understand and accept him for who he is. In this scenario, Mark's awareness of his triggers allows him to adapt his approach to networking, not just avoid it altogether, ultimately leading to a more positive and fulfilling experience.

The goal of overcoming social fear isn't to try and fight your social anxiety, but to learn to accept, understand, and manage it. True confidence doesn't come from trying to be somebody you're not; it comes from acknowledging the things that scare you and creating a strategy to push through them. By embracing your fears and actively working to overcome them, you're well on your way to No Fear Networking, sweaty armpits and all.

Create a Plan That Feels Challenging but Possible

If you haven't guessed by now, I'm a big fan of baby steps and slow and steady growth. This method is all about slowly ramping up your exposure to networking scenarios, ensuring each step feels doable, and not like you're jumping into the deep end and flailing without a life jacket. It's about testing the water, and then, when you're ready, swimming with confidence.

First, consider what your goals are for networking. What do you want to get out of this? Is it finding a mentor? Learning about new job opportunities? Growing your sphere of influence? Learning how to participate in small talk without wanting to throw up the dozen cocktail weenies you shoveled down from the hors d'oeuvres table?

Having clear objectives will give you not only a direction but also a way to measure your progress.

Second, find what suits you. One of the biggest misconceptions about networking is that it must be done in one very specific way.

Networking is, by definition, "the action or process of interacting with others to exchange information and develop professional or social contacts."[5] So let's chuck out the notion that networking has to be this stiff affair with suits, high tables, and awkward small talk circles.

The key here is to find what works best for you and lean into it. For me, I'm all about those smaller, cozy gatherings – think 10 people max. I shine in online spaces and crave a bit of structure, where everyone knows why they're there and what they're talking about. It saves me from diving into a monolog about the deliciousness of the cheese platter. I also prefer to sit down rather than stand around. It's leagues away from the stiffness of stand-up mingling where I silently curse at myself for wearing heels instead of my beloved Birkenstocks.

Given my inclination toward smaller groups, structured interactions, online engagement, and the comfort of seated discussions, my approach to networking could look something like this:

I research different conferences in my industry, landing on something like Social Media Marketing World in San Diego. Coming from Ottawa, the idea of jetting off to San Diego has its share of butterflies but also screams adventure (plus, I discover that they stuff burritos with french fries, so it's a no-brainer, really).

I looked up the itinerary. They have some bigger parties, which may not be my jam, but they also have forums where people can create meetups at coffee shops or dinner near the conference center based on their interests. Bingo! A pre-conference coffee hangout for female entrepreneurs. Plus, tapping into a Facebook group for attendees pre-event means I'm warming up before even setting foot there. Lastly, I notice that they do roundtable talks at lunch and I can volunteer to host one. I can choose the conversation topic and questions and have people join me. This feels challenging but doable for me. By the conference end, I'm buzzing with energy, not zapped from trying to fit into the traditional networking mold and feeling like a failure because I needed something a bit different to thrive.

Take a moment to think about some unique networking environments that feel like a challenge but also kind of fun. That's your socialization sweet spot.

Practice, Practice, Practice

The last step on this journey of overcoming social fear is to do the hard things again and again. Remember that networking does not equal a traditional reception hall buzzing with strangers. Opportunities to work on your networking skills are everywhere, from a brief elevator ride to standing in line at the grocery store, even to the moments you're waiting in the Starbucks drive-thru.

Battling social anxiety is a feat in itself, and for someone like me, who is both socially anxious and introverted, the challenge doubles. I recharge with alone time, which, if I'm not careful, can lead to entire weekends spent in the comfort of my couch.

The temptation to remain within our comfort zones is stronger than ever, too. In an era where our televisions and smartphones promise endless entertainment and socialization without ever needing to step outside, it can be easy to fall into the trap of believing that this is true.

One habit that I've created and stuck to for years is the rule of one social interaction per day. No matter what deadlines I'm trying to meet or which TV show is premiering, it's nonnegotiable for me to step outside my home and connect with someone I've never met before.

There are days when this means opting to walk into a coffee shop instead of making my order through an app, or choosing to visit a bank in person rather than depositing a check at an ATM. These choices might be less convenient at the moment, but they play a pivotal role in my journey toward managing my social anxiety in the long run.

As you continue to practice, you'll find that your social fears start to diminish, not because the situations themselves have changed, but because *you've* changed. You've built resilience, confidence, and skills through consistent practice. This journey is not about trying to erase fear completely but more about learning to navigate it with self-compassion, understanding, and courage.

So embrace the practice. Remember, each step forward, no matter how small, is a step toward a more confident, socially awesome you.

Strategies for Building Confidence When You Walk into a Room

For me, the boss level for the socially anxious professional like you and me is the traditional networking reception. Even just writing that years ago would have truly made me shudder as I typed. Today, it feels much like other social situations. Can it be overstimulating and overwhelming at times? Of course, but it feels nothing like it used to in my body, thanks to strategies that I've learned and used to overcome that initial urge to run far, far away.

So without further ado, here are some things that I've learned going from agoraphobic hermit to public speaker (which, unfortunately, involves human interaction – it's part of the gig).

Lesson 1: Think About Where You Will Be Before and After the Event

For events happening away from home, consider where you will be pre- and post-event. Why? Because for somebody with social anxiety, being able to mentally and physically prepare before a social event can be incredibly helpful.

When I first started speaking, I used to stay at the hotel hosting the event or whichever hotel was close by. While sometimes I still do this if necessary, some of my absolute favorite conferences have been ones where instead of staying on site, I found a fun little rental nearby, but not right in the thick of it.

For me, having more distance took some of the pressure off because I wasn't always feeling the need to be "on." I could order nachos at 1 a.m. and grab the takeout bag outside in my PJs without worrying about somebody seeing me in my fuzzy slippers. I knew that once I was finished networking and needed to recharge, I could relax and unwind in a place that felt more like home than a cold hotel room.

If you know that you may be battling butterflies beforehand, or need a sanctuary to nap in post-event, try considering where you want your home base to be.

Lesson 2: Have a Game Day Ritual

A reception hall might not resemble a Super Bowl stadium, but to someone with social anxiety, it can certainly feel just as intimidating! That's exactly why it's crucial to approach these situations as if you're an athlete gearing up for the big game.

Having a game day ritual has been so helpful for me to walk into a room feeling like I'm about to score a touchdown. Early on in my career, I would rush from work straight to an event, and be out of breath when I got there. I would just chalk up my nervous energy to my social anxiety, when really it was because I hadn't prepared myself properly and gotten into the right mindset to feel calm and ready.

Nowadays, if I know I'll be attending a networking event, I try to get a good rest beforehand, hop into a warm shower, and then tackle my hair and makeup with an energizing playlist (think lots of 2000s girly pop). Before I leave for the event, I meditate for 10 minutes and take deep breaths with a stress release spray that helps to ground me. I put on my "going out" perfume because it seems to signal to my brain that I'm entering socialization mode.

Walking out the door, I carry with me not just the anticipation of the connections I'll make but also a slice of peace that I've created. It's my personal pregame warmup that ensures I arrive not just physically prepared, but mentally ready to make the most of the networking opportunity ahead. No longer out of breath or frazzled, I step into the room with a calm confidence, ready to tackle whatever comes my way, one conversation at a time.

Now, I'm curious about you. What could your pre-event ritual look like? Whether it's a specific song that gets you in the right mindset, a lucky charm you always carry, or a moment of silence to collect your thoughts, having a routine that gets you mentally in the best space possible is undoubtedly a game changer.

Now, sometimes having a game day ritual also means embracing something a little daunting — setting, dare I say, boundaries. Cue the ominous horror movie soundtrack.

As I began speaking more on stages, I began to notice something. I would show up early to meet and greet people, step on stage to perform, and by the time I got off stage, I would feel physically exhausted.

This made networking and answering questions tough, and would give people the impression that I wasn't engaged or interested in conversations. That's when it clicked: my social battery has a two-hour lifespan.

Realizing this was pivotal, especially since my keynotes typically span an hour. To ensure I had enough energy to connect with people post-talk, I had to make a strategic decision to conserve my social energy beforehand.

Not every professional with social anxiety is introverted. However, for those who relate to having a short social battery life like I do, recognizing and planning around your capacity is crucial. For me, this meant having to decline pre-event social invitations such as breakfasts, lunches, or gatherings at the hotel bar. This wasn't about being antisocial; I wish I could do it all.

It was about ensuring I could bring my best self to the stage and remain genuinely present for conversations afterward.

Lesson 3: Know What You're Getting Yourself into (Literally!)

I'm a data girl. When my husband and I were planning a trip to Hawaii, I asked him for the address of the resort. First, I started researching the resort: the rooms, the pool, the restaurants, the normal stuff. Then I started looking around the resort at which restaurants and shopping was nearby.

Then I took a sharp turn into crazy town because I didn't just start looking at the beaches nearby; I started researching which beaches on the island had the most and least number of shark attacks.

But here's the weirdest part of all: this exercise made me calm. The data soothed my anxiety rather than increased it. My mind thrives on being able to paint a detailed picture of what to expect and understanding the risks involved. That's why, whenever we're dining out, I'm the one who knows exactly what I'll order well before we step through the restaurant's doors – and odds are, it won't be seafood.

Why does this matter to you? Because visualization can be a powerful tool when it comes to networking with social anxiety. Just as I find comfort and calm in carefully planning and researching every detail of a trip, you too can harness the power of visualization to ease into social situations more confidently.

First, imagine the venue. Usually, you can visit a website where you can see the venue yourself or a blueprint of it. If not, you can ask the organizer for more information on what to expect when you get there. Think of any details that may feel uncomfortable – parking, registration, where to leave your coat – so that you're able to paint a full picture of what the experience might be like. Heck, if you're really struggling, go visit the venue beforehand and take a quick peek. The goal is to attend the event with confidence, so do what you need to do to make that happen!

Next, imagine successful interactions with others at the event. Social anxiety tends to serve you visualizations of the worst-case scenarios, so it's time to consciously counter that with positive ones. Think about how you might introduce yourself and topics that you might want to discuss. Imagine the dialogue flowing effortlessly, as if you're chatting with an old friend or a close family member. Visualize yourself discovering exciting opportunities and exchanging contact information with new people.

This visualization strategy will arm you with the tools to stride into networking events feeling prepared and calm, transforming what might seem like an intimidating challenge into a smooth, fearless experience.

Embracing Vulnerability in Professional Relationships

Are you still with me? I know, mentioning "vulnerability" and "professional" in the same breath often sends people scrambling, yet believe it or not, vulnerability is the cornerstone of genuine networking. In fact, one of the main reasons many find small talk challenging (a topic we'll explore further) is its lack of this essential ingredient for forging authentic connections.

Before exploring the role of vulnerability in professional settings, it's important to clarify what vulnerability actually means, given its sometimes bad reputation. For this, let's turn to the renowned expert on vulnerability, courage, shame, and empathy, Brené Brown. She articulates vulnerability as "uncertainty, risk, and emotional exposure."[6] At its heart, being vulnerable means being willing to present your true self, imperfections and all.

To clarify this even further, understand that this does not give you a free pass to show up to the next networking reception in your undies and say, "Michaela told me to be vulnerable!" or to post about your colonoscopy on LinkedIn.

Navigating the line between vulnerability and oversharing is crucial in a professional context; while the former can foster connection and understanding, the latter may lead to discomfort and disconnection. The appropriateness of what's shared often hinges not just on the content, but on the context and its relevance to the work environment.

Scenario 1: Embracing Vulnerability to Motivate the Team

Sarah's team was on edge, facing a looming deadline amid constant changes requested by the client. The air was thick with tension during their final meeting, with team members voicing concerns about meeting the deadline.

Acknowledging the frustration, Sarah shared, "I understand your frustration; I'm feeling it too. We're in a tough spot, and it's a hard challenge. I've faced similar situations before, questioning if it was possible. And yet here I am, having managed to overcome those challenges. It was far from easy, but it was possible. Together, we can tackle this one too."

She then invited her team to share their own experiences of overcoming difficult situations. This gesture, coupled with a brief coffee break, rekindled the team's spirit. They returned to their tasks, reenergized by Sarah's empathy and reassured by her leadership.

Scenario 2: The Impact of Oversharing on Team Dynamics

In a parallel universe, Sarah observed the same discouragement and tension among her team members due to the demanding project and tight deadline.

Seeking to connect on a personal level, Sarah opted to share her current personal struggle, saying, "I get your frustration, truly. On a personal note, I'm dealing with something challenging – my relationship with my husband has been so bad lately, and it's been tough to concentrate on work. It's like everything's falling apart."

What was intended as a moment of connection spiraled into an hour-long discussion about her personal life, leaving the team in an awkward position of providing emotional support rather than focusing on the project.

Post-meeting, the team's energy was noticeably diminished. Conversations by the coffee machine revealed discomfort with the oversharing, and the team's focus had shifted from the project deadline to Sarah's personal issues.

These scenarios underscore the importance of discerning between vulnerability that serves to build understanding and trust within a team, and oversharing that may inadvertently create discomfort and distraction.

As Brene Brown puts it, "Vulnerability is based on mutuality and requires boundaries and trust. It's not oversharing, it's not purging, it's not indiscriminate disclosure, and it's not celebrity-style social media information dumps. Vulnerability is about sharing our feelings and our experiences with people who have earned the right to hear them."[7]

Following are some of the ways that you can embrace vulnerability in your professional life without oversharing.

Share Personal Experiences and Challenges   Remember that sharing personal experiences in a professional setting isn't about an open floodgate of personal life details. Instead, it's about selectively sharing relevant things that humanize you to your colleagues or clients. When you do so, you pave the way for others to also open up and create an environment that feels safe and welcoming.

April Roberts, founder of the exclusive mastermind for Gen X female founders called Vixen Gathering, puts it beautifully: "I found that usually if you go first and you're vulnerable, it sets the stage for other people too. So, when networking or in client meetings, I would share why a topic is important to me, or an insight I've gained. Then, we'd go around the table. It's like you want to give before you get – the same concept applies here."[8]

Just make sure that whatever you are sharing ties back to the topic at hand and provides wisdom, support, or inspiration to the person that you're speaking with.

Still not entirely sure what, and how much, to disclose? Dr. Carole Robin's "15% rule" suggests that when we push ourselves to share a little more than we're comfy with, about 15% beyond our usual openness, it can set the conditions for making stronger connections.

This kind of sharing not only helps others get a better understanding of us, but also invites them to make themselves better known to us. This kind of reciprocal vulnerability also creates a space where genuine relationships can blossom more easily. Think of it as upgrading incrementally from small talk to meaningful conversations.[9]

This approach isn't just helpful in personal growth but is a total game changer in professional and educational environments too.

Ask for Help or Advice   If sharing more of who you are still feels scary, try asking for help or advice. Seeking guidance fosters trust by showing humility, honesty, and a willingness to listen to and learn from others. So often, we are taught that competence means having all the answers, when really it's actually the ability to do something well. You cannot be great without growth, and growth requires learning, so start asking!

Show Gratitude   One of the simplest ways to incorporate more vulnerability into your professional relationships is to say thanks.

Sure, I'd toss out a "thanks" when someone wrapped up a task, but deep down, I was feeling so much gratitude for the people around me and never really voiced it. Then one evening, stuck in traffic and lost in thought, it hit me:

> "I spend most days not hearing that anybody appreciates me, and I bet others do too."

It was a tiny moment, but man, did it stick with me. That's when I kicked it up a notch with the compliments and made it a point to express my gratitude more openly.

I also moved beyond just thanking people for the tasks they did; I started telling them, "Thank you so much, I appreciate you." Those words, "I appreciate you," became something I'd say often to make sure people knew I valued them for who they were, not just for what they did for me.

Every year around the holidays in December, I also record videos to send to those who have impacted my life. Nothing fancy, just a quick selfie video to say thank you and to share a specific thing that they did that impacted my year. These messages are my way of saying, "You've made a difference in my life," something that people don't hear often enough, if at all.

Showing gratitude sets the tone for genuine, reciprocal connections where appreciation goes beyond surface-level "so, the weather…" interactions.

And beyond fostering deeper connections, embracing vulnerability has an unexpected advantage for managing your social anxiety. When you drop the mask of polished perfection and you allow people to see you more as who you really are, you also are courageously challenging the narratives crafted by social anxiety.

A few years ago, very early on as a speaker, I was asked to speak at an event. Talking in front of crowds wasn't new to me, but this time they wanted me to dive into my battles with agoraphobia. I was moving on up in my career, and talking about a perceived weakness felt dangerous and scary.

I had never spoken about it publicly before. I had only talked about it with a select few people in my life, ever. But it was a great opportunity on a big stage and could be a big break for me.

So I took the plunge. I spent the weeks leading up to the event hammering out my speech, heart racing every time I ran through it. The thought of sharing my story, out loud and proud, was petrifying.

Then came the night. There I was, spotlight on me, with an audience mid-dinner, casually enjoying their soup as I approached the podium, hands shaking. With a deep breath, I began.

"I still remember my first anxiety attack…" My voice was a giveaway of my nerves. A quick throat clear, and I carried on with my agoraphobia experience, eyes glued to my notes, praying for it to be over.

But when I dared to look up, expecting judgment, I found none. Just women and men in business casual attire, still sipping their soup, as if life stories like mine were what they came to hear. No gasps, no dropped spoons – nothing. The nightmare scenario I'd built up in my mind was just that, a story I was telling myself.

When I got off stage, several people came over to me, not to judge or ridicule me, but to congratulate me and share their own stories of social anxiety and agoraphobia.

So those stories in your head? The ones saying you've got to hide who you really are or else you won't fit in? Well, they've got it all wrong. When you let your guard down and show your true colors, you're inadvertently also proving that those fears are bogus. What's more is that you also open yourself up to deeper conversations, and through others you realize that you are not alone in those social anxiety created thoughts.

And knowing that you are not alone, as corny as it sounds, is easily the greatest gift of networking.

4 | Developing a Magnetic Personal Brand

If "networking" hasn't already sent you searching for a cozy cave to hibernate in, then "personal brand" might just have you tapping into your inner mountain goat, ready to scale the nearest peak of solitude.

Trust me, I get it.

It's a buzzword that gives the same energy as "leveraging synergy to disrupt the ecosystem and pivot with a holistic approach to address pain points." In other words, it can come off as insincere and reduce you to feeling like a product or service.

But here's the thing: no matter what terminology you use, what we're actually talking about is not about *selling* yourself. It's about *sharing* yourself.

Why Do You Need a Personal Brand for Networking?

Personal branding is less about a sales strategy and more about presenting what you care about, narrating your career journey in an engaging way, and clarifying your goals and how others might support you in achieving them.

It's not a playbook on manipulation; it's about making your professional journey more relatable and inviting people along for the ride.

My own encounter with what I'd come to recognize as my personal brand happened unexpectedly in 2016. At 29, entrenched in the hustle of a local tech startup, I was so buried in work that my car's backseat often seemed a more practical bedroom than my actual home. Then one morning my world turned on its head when my boss, accompanied by the HR rep, ushered me into a meeting room for an unexpected chat.

Well, shit.

He mumbled a few things about my dedication and hard work before slipping me a paper to sign that read, in full caps and a bold font: **LAYOFF NOTICE**.

I had never faced a layoff or firing before. I quickly signed the form, my cheeks burning with shame. As I scribbled my signature, I could feel the weight of my colleagues' stares – pity, concern, fear of being next.

I bolted out of the office, raced to my car, and put my head against the steering wheel. "What am I going to do now?" I thought to myself.

With nothing left to lose, I took to LinkedIn, not with a resume but with a declaration. I'd been laid off, and I was determined to find my next opportunity through the power of community on that very platform. I wasn't going to send out a resume, but I was going to network my way to my next big gig instead.

What followed was nothing short of miraculous. My post spiraled into a whirlwind of shares and messages, job leads from strangers, and tales of layoffs flooding my inbox. I was bewildered. Why did my story resonate so deeply with so many I had never met?

The answer dawned on me: it wasn't just my story – they saw a piece of their journey in mine. Their cheeks had burned too; they had also felt that stomach churn that comes after hearing, "Can I speak with you in my office?"

So I committed to daily posts, sharing candid stories from my job hunt. Within weeks, I was juggling job offers and racing between interviews. Eventually, I snagged a great marketing position at a local IT firm that they created for me after seeing my posts, a victory I shared on LinkedIn.

That post exploded across LinkedIn, reaching millions and catching the attention of major publications.

The experience was intoxicating – not the viral fame (that part was honestly terrifying), but the realization that I was crafting something far greater than a job title. In mere weeks, I had fostered a community that valued me for who I was, not just for the roles I filled. They connected with me for sharing the most authentic gift I could offer – myself.

This experience unveiled a powerful truth: the essence of a personal brand is not in becoming a product; it's about turning your story into your strongest professional asset. This profound realization didn't just alter my career trajectory; it underscored the impact of genuine, personal connection in the professional realm that can often feel cold and impersonal.

In a noisy world filled with mass-produced business cards and stacks of resumes, standing out is more important than ever. Differentiating yourself in a sea of competition relies on the power of a personal brand.

And here's the thing: *you already have a personal brand.* Your LinkedIn profile, the way you introduce yourself at events, the outfit you wear to a team meeting, everything that you do or say or wear tells a story.

It's the impression that you leave behind. It's the echo of your interactions, the whispers of your presence long after you've left the room.

Your personal brand is simply how you make people feel and becomes a magnet that draws others to you.

One of the things that motivated me to start sharing on LinkedIn was that I was tired of being reduced to a resume. I wasn't born rich or famous, I was (and am) a regular person from Ottawa, Canada, which, in case you're wondering, is known as Canada's "most boring city"[1] and not for its pulsating creative scenes. I felt like if I could just get to know people outside my Ottawa bubble, maybe there would be more out there for me.

This drive wasn't born out of ambition for fame or a desire to become someone I'm not. It was about breaking free from the box that seemed to confine me, and leveling the playing field. LinkedIn did just that, turning my stage from a small-town karaoke bar to a worldwide arena. It was as if suddenly I was handed a microphone and my voice mattered.

Even more important, people remembered my voice. Suddenly, I was networking with much more ease, because people recognized me and my stories, which made small talk flow because we had familiarity and a starting point in conversations.

And here's the real magic: visibility leads to opportunity. The more I shared, the more I found myself offered opportunities that were previously unimaginable. Job offers, speaking engagements, and collaborations started to pour in from corners of the world I'd never been to. Each post, each story, each shared piece of my journey was like a beacon, drawing people closer.

It hasn't been easy.

I had spent nearly three decades trying to shrink myself, so the idea of opening up online to millions of strangers across the world was not necessarily part of my hermit blueprint. Yet, with every share, every nudge of the "post" button, I felt a little bit braver.

With every story, every snippet of my life that I put out there, I found pieces of myself growing bolder, stronger, and more visible.

Do you need to post on LinkedIn to build your personal brand? Absolutely not. Your chosen platform is irrelevant; it's about building a presence, whether online or offline or both, that creates trust, resonates with your audience, and most importantly, gives you the courage to walk into any room like you own it.

Crafting Your Professional Story

"I hate talking about myself." Over and over, I hear the same challenge from my clients. Many of them are successful businesswomen, senior executives with resumes that would make your jaw drop.

But whenever we start talking about what they've done, their successes, their career history, there's a visible squirming. It's like self-promotion doesn't quite fit with who they are, and feels more like a flex than simply stating the truth.

This feeling, "I hate talking about myself," isn't just a minor hurdle. It's a reflection of a deeper struggle that many face in the professional world (especially women, who have been conditioned to underplay their success to fit into societal norms, but that's another book for another day).

It also represents a symptom of imposter syndrome, which is "a behavioral health phenomenon described as self-doubt of intellect, skills, or accomplishments among high-achieving individuals."[2]

So, in plain language, what's that all about?

Imposter syndrome is like having this annoying worry that you don't really deserve the good things happening to you. It's like there's a voice in your head constantly saying it's all due to luck or just being in the right place at the right time, not because you're actually good enough. Imposter syndrome gives you a terrible feeling that any moment now, everyone's going to realize you're just faking it and all your shortcomings are going to be exposed.

For me, imposter syndrome kicked in pretty early. I can trace it back to grade school, believe it or not. I had this wild idea in my head that maybe my classmates were being paid to hang out with me. It sounds ridiculous now, but back then it felt totally real. I was always on edge, waiting for someone to jump out and say, "Surprise! We all think you're a total loser, and your mom has to bribe us to pretend otherwise!"

As I got older, it didn't go away. In university, I'd get my exams back and immediately check the name, just to be sure they hadn't mixed mine up with someone else's who actually knew what they were doing.

When I started job hunting and began getting offers, I'd hurry to sign them before the employers realized they meant to hire someone else, someone who was obviously more qualified than I was.

And if we're getting super real here, even with this book, imposter syndrome was right there with me. With so many incredible writers out there, were they sure they picked the right person? Despite all my hard work and dreaming about this moment, it still felt like maybe the publisher made a big mistake.

This isn't just a consequence. In a study of 247 participants,[3] researchers found a medium to strong correlation between society anxiety levels and imposter syndrome expressions among the students. So, if you are a socially anxious professional, chances are you can relate to this nagging feeling that you aren't enough.

But, to rock the hell out of your professional story, this is something that we need to tackle. Otherwise, whenever you sit down to write your career story, it will feel like a painful, impossible task. Think about it. How can you confidently share your accomplishments and milestones when there's a mosquito buzzing around your ear telling you that you didn't deserve it?

The true challenge in crafting your professional story, then, isn't so much about writing skills or finding the time to put pen to paper — it's deeper than that (but you already knew that, didn't you?).

So let's dive into eight steps to sculpt your professional story:

Look Imposter Syndrome Square in the Eye

The first step to crafting your professional story is to recognize the biggest roadblock that may be standing in your way, feeling uncomfortable talking about yourself or your accomplishments.

There are multiple ways to combat feelings of inadequacy. First, remember that your discomfort is not a sign of incompetency. Imposter syndrome is a phenomenon that affects many. Up to 82% of people also experience feelings of being an imposter.[4] If you belong to an underrepresented group, such as BIPOC or members of the LGBTQ2S+ communities, imposter syndrome is even more prominent, pointing to factors beyond just the person, and on a wider cultural/societal level.

As a biracial woman, I can relate to this. A big part of my own imposter syndrome growing up was that I have blonde hair, hazel eyes, light skin, and a Black father. My late dad was born and raised in Port of Spain, Trinidad, and immigrated to Canada in his adulthood to pursue a medical degree.

I am one of seven siblings, and I am, by far, the most white passing of the bunch. Growing up, I struggled with feeling like my exterior didn't match my identity. Classmates would share racist jokes, and I would either have to correct them and "out" myself as biracial, or hang my head and absorb the toxic sentiments that my family and I were less than. I've always felt like I am wearing a mask, presenting as a white woman but internally a proud mixed daughter, a feeling that I'm sure you can relate to if you belong to a group that is underrepresented.

As you can see, imposter syndrome is so much bigger than just some toxic thoughts you have about yourself. It is a common feeling that spans across humankind, and is even more pronounced in those in underrepresented communities, those who also battle social anxiety or other neurodivergent conditions, and also people who are generally high achievers.

Another way to combat imposter syndrome is to list out the facts. Pause and take a deep breath. Really think about the journey you've been on. The late nights studying, the blood, sweat, and tears, the challenges faced head on. These aren't just minor things; they're milestones that mark your path to where you stand today. It's easy to get caught up in the whirlwind of daily tasks and forget just how far you've come.

But let's take it a step further. Grab a pen and paper, or open a new note on your phone, and start jotting down everything it took to get you where you are now. Start with the tangible achievements: degrees earned, jobs you've scored, projects completed, awards received. Then, dig deeper. Write about the skills you developed along the way, and the personal growth you experienced for each accomplishment.

This exercise may not feel comfy, but it's hard to dismiss your worth and question your capabilities when you're faced with a paper record of your own experiences and achievements. It's a reminder that you didn't get to where you are by accident or mere "luck and timing." You are here because of your efforts, your choices, and your grit.

Another way to combat imposter syndrome is by sharing with others. Say out loud those wild imposter thoughts your brain's been brewing. Pretend you're speaking to a friend and share it. It sounds pretty silly out loud, doesn't it?

- "I only got my job because I was wearing a shirt to the interview that was my boss's favorite color."
- "I have this fear that one day there's going to be a surprise exam where everyone realizes I'm not actually qualified and I'll be fired."
- "Any second now, everyone will realize I've been Googling half my job and so I have to be friendly with everybody at work because when they figure it out, hopefully they'll like me so much that they'll let me keep working here."
- "I only got this speaking gig because every other speaker must have turned it down first."

I, absolutely, totally, have *not* had these thoughts myself and they are definitely made up (wink, wink).

Recently, a LinkedIn connection asked me how I overcame imposter syndrome, and I replied that while I still get little nagging whispers from time to time, by far the most powerful way to shut down imposter syndrome is to openly share your thoughts and feelings with people that you trust to be vulnerable with.

When we voice these fears, we often find that others have been harboring similar thoughts, which instantly reduces their grip. The more we talk about imposter thoughts, the more we understand how common these feelings are, regardless of how successful we appear on the outside. That moment that you discover that everyone's winging it to some degree? It's like a weight being lifted off your shoulders.

As Sarah Wilson noted in her book *First, We Make the Beast Beautiful: A New Journey Through Anxiety*, "There's a lot of solace in knowing there are others out there experiencing what you are…you can share your insecurities and in turn gain new ways to cope."[5]

Another way to face down your imposter syndrome is to find people like you.

When I first started speaking, I would share my bloopers on LinkedIn – not as pity bait, but because I wanted to hold myself accountable to keep going. One day, a good friend of mine, whom I love but who has a vastly different online presence than mine, pulled me aside and gave me this advice:

> "If you want to get the big gigs, you only need to share your highlight reel. Event planners don't want imperfect speakers."

It stung. I knew that it came from a place of love and wanting me to succeed, but it made me question whether there was even a place for a socially anxious speaker. I had gone from agoraphobia to trying to make it on stage, and maybe the spotlight wasn't for people like me.

So, for a while, I stopped sharing the hard stuff. I looked at what other speakers were wearing on stage and tried to copy their outfits. So often, I felt like I was cosplaying as a public speaker instead of being one.

For me, the only way out of this was to seek out speakers who were like me, those who were openly sharing their struggles with social anxiety and awkwardness, but absolutely crushing it anyway.

I also look for events where there are multiple female speakers. It's common in the speaking industry to see events with a lineup of almost all white male speakers, with one or two females or BIPOC experts sprinkled in just to avoid criticism. I don't have interest in participating in events where I feel like my voice doesn't belong.

By surrounding myself with people who inspired me rather than made me feel out of place, I learned to view my journey through a lens of compassion and pride, rather than criticism and comparison. So, if you're feeling like an imposter, remember you're in good company.

The key to battling imposter syndrome isn't to silence the doubts but to speak them out loud, to share them, and to find others who are facing similar challenges. Imposter syndrome thrives on silence and solitude, so every time we give voice to our fears, we chip away at the power they hold.

Reflect on Your Career Journey So Far

Have you ever found yourself fumbling over your words when someone casually asks, "So, tell me about yourself," during a chat or in the middle of an interview? It sounds straightforward enough, but somehow you end up feeling like you've been thrown a curveball in a pop quiz you didn't know we were taking. But why is that?

In both our personal and professional lives, there's a relentless push toward the next big thing – your next vacation spot, the upcoming promotion, snagging a new job, or signing that next client. Ambition is our modern-day mantra, and rightly so. However, what often gets sidelined in this hustle is the art of reflection.

As the late, great Maya Angelou once said, "You can't really know where you're going until you know where you have been."[6]

Reflection helps you connect the dots of your career story more clearly. I used to struggle to quickly summarize my journey because it all felt so disjointed and random. I've been everything from a mascot dressed as a can of beans for Mardi Gras to a director of marketing, and it almost felt embarrassing to detail the zigzag of my career. But the more time I spent reflecting on my past roles, the more I realized that it was no small coincidence that I was attracted to positions where I could perform, create, or teach.

As you go through this process of reflection, you'll probably also notice recurring themes in your career. Maybe you've loved jobs that gave you a chance to solve problems, or make a lasting positive impact on the environment, or manage projects or people.

These are clues to your true passions and purpose. Recognizing them can help you understand what drives you, guiding you toward opportunities that fulfill you deeply. So let's take a moment here and really dig into this with a quick exercise. Grab a sheet of paper, open a drawing file on your computer or phone, or simply visualize this in your mind. Ready? Here we go:

- Start by sketching a timeline that spans from the start of your career to your current status. Picture it as a straightforward line running from point A, the beginning, to point B, today.
- Now, using one color, mark dots on the line representing key moments (different jobs, personal life milestones, promotions, new

projects, whatever feels important to you). Write down what drew you to that key moment. For example, why did you decide to accept a new position or promotion, why did you decide to have kids, get married, or move to a new city?

- Now jot down all of the highlights above the line, the good stuff that's happened and what you learned from it. Also include the knee-scraping failure moments below the line, and don't forget to jot down those lessons too.

- Step back and look at your timeline. What themes stand out to you? Which milestones brought you the most fulfillment and why? As you answer these questions, also consider what the ideal future looks like based on what has brought you the most joy so far in your life and career. Write that down too.

This exercise is not just about mapping out your past but about connecting the dots in a way that guides you toward a future rich in fulfillment and joy, and being able to clearly communicate it all!

Embrace Your True North Traits

As I was considering this step in sculpting your professional story, I felt uninspired by the idea of just plain old skills. Sure, reflecting on the things that you're uniquely skilled in, like writing or accounting, is helpful, but it doesn't feel like quite enough when you're trying to craft your professional story. Then it came to me as I was sipping on my double-double from Tim Hortons: you need to consider which skills are your True North Traits.

True North Traits are the innate talents, skills, and virtue that are deeply intertwined with your identity at your core. They aren't just something that you do; they are who you are, like being a problem solver, a people connector, or the person who always lends a hand without a second thought. Your True North traits go beyond just your talents and skills because they also act like a beacon, guiding your actions, interactions, and decisions, and steering you in the direction that your inner self feels called to.

Here are some questions to ask yourself to discover and embrace your True North Traits:

Talents: Talents are your default settings, the things you do instinctively well. These are things that feel as natural to you as breathing. Here are some questions to uncover yours:

- When do I feel most like myself?
- What am I doing when I lose track of time?
- What do I find super easy that seems to be challenging for everyone else?
- Back in the school days, what subjects did I crush without even trying?

Skills: Skills are the tricks you've got in your toolkit, honed and polished through practice, and maybe a little blood, sweat, and tears. Here are some questions to unlock your greatest skills:

- What gets me out of bed faster than a double shot of espresso?
- What could I talk about for hours on end without needing a nap?
- For the challenges I've overcome, what specific skills did I rely on to navigate through them?
- When have I been the go-to person for something? What was I offering?

Virtues: Virtues are qualities that you choose to embody every day of your life. They aren't talents you're born with or skills you develop; they are woven deep into the fabric of your character. Your skills and talents may be the wind that pushes you forward, but your virtues are the compass that guides the way. Here are some questions to ask yourself as you reflect on your virtues:

- In what environments do I thrive the most?
- What values do I stand for, and how do they show up in my life and work?
- What's the cause that gets me on my soapbox, even if I'm normally reserved?
- Who are my heroes, and what traits do we share?

Like you did earlier with your career journey, take a step back and identify patterns that have emerged when reflecting on your True North Traits. Look for the constellations in your reflections on True North Traits. This introspection isn't just about identifying what you're good at; it's about really being intentional about connecting the dots of who you are.

Not only will this help guide you on the career path that aligns with your core being, but it will help you to clearly and effectively communicate with the next person that asks you to share a bit about yourself, so you won't just recite a list of jobs and hobbies. This way, you turn every introduction into an opportunity to showcase the best, truest version of you.

Draft and Polish It

Good news! If that reflection practice was hard and uncomfy, it truly is the hardest part of crafting your professional story, I promise!

Now it's time to piece together those insights from your career journey and True North Traits into a draft that's still a bit messy. Jot down key moments, achievements, challenges, and turning points in your career, anything that feels relevant.

For the brainstorming stage, don't worry about making it pretty. Here you want to just let it flow and you can cut down the unnecessary bits afterward. If you don't know how to start writing, one easy tip is to start by recording your voice on your phone and then transcribing it.

When you feel like you've gotten it all down, it's time to polish it into a more cohesive narrative. Here's a format that I recommend to capture all of you:

Who I Am: Unpacking My True North Traits

This isn't about what's on your business card or your LinkedIn profile. This is about peeling back the layers to reveal what makes you *you*. Refer back to your career timeline and share stories and milestones that shine a light on these traits, showing not just what you're made of but how these qualities are who you are.

Why I Do What I Do: My True North in Action

Here's where things get fun. How did your inner compass direct you in your career? Maybe it's your deep-rooted empathy that naturally nudged you toward a career in helping others, or your strategic, analytical mind that found its calling in the ever-changing world of tech. Show how your inner strengths and virtues light up every step you take in your work.

How I Make a Difference

Focus on your impact more than the job description. This isn't just a list of duties or your accomplishments. Instead, detail how your work serves others or impacts the world around you. Remember that the person you're speaking to may want to work with you or buy from you so focus your attention on how you can help them.

What I Want to Do Next

Finally, gaze into the future. Where do you see yourself going? Dream big and don't be afraid to share those dreams with others. People are drawn to those who are ambitious and courageous enough to voice those big dreams. But make sure it ties back to your sections on who you are, why you do what you do, and how you make a difference.

Once you're finished shaping your words into sections, go back and edit. You want to make sure that it doesn't feel like just a bio; it should feel conversational because you'll be using this story in social interactions. Aim for a tone that feels like you're sharing your story with a friend. It should be natural and engaging, ready to be shared in social settings.

Imagine speaking to somebody in front of you. Read it out loud. Does it sound like you're speaking directly to them? If it still feels a bit stiff, it's time for another round of edits to ensure it truly reflects your voice and feels as natural and engaging as a chat over coffee.

Extract Your Story Snippet

Now that you've got your polished story, it's time to distill a shortened version of it for those moments that you only need a story snippet. If you haven't guessed by now, I'm a coffee lover, so I like to think of this as a strong espresso shot, where your longer version is like a rich, equally delicious Americano.

Here's how to do it. First, identify the core of the story. For example, I once had a client who was a successful event planner. As we chatted about her life and career journey, she shared a story about how when she was a little girl, instead of trying to sell lemonade from a stand, she would go door to door and ask her neighbors if she could organize their closet for a dollar.

I immediately noticed the connection between her love of organization and project management and her current love for event planning. So, zeroing in on that core, the love for organization and project management that's been a constant from her childhood into her career, is crucial to her story snippet because it incorporates her True North Traits perfectly into the present. Here's what her story snippet using that core might look like:

> *Ever since I was a kid, hustling door-to-door not to sell lemonade but to organize closets for a dollar, I've had a knack for transforming chaos into order.*
>
> *That passion for organization wasn't just a childhood quirk; it was the early signs of what would become my life's work.*
>
> *Fast forward to today, and I'm channeling that same love for meticulous planning and creative solutions into my career as an event planner.*
>
> *Each event is a puzzle, and I thrive on piecing it together, turning every vision into beautiful moments that people cherish forever. And yes, I still do love a well-organized closet, if you're wondering!*

Here you can see that we tied an early life story that demonstrated some True North Traits, connected them to her current and future endeavors, but didn't lose her funny, warm personality in the process.

Make sure as you distill to create your story snippet that you don't lose the voice and tone of your original piece. If you aren't sure, read both out loud once you're finished to make sure that they have the same vibe.

Ask for Feedback

For a professional with social anxiety, writing can feel much easier than sharing, but this part is so crucial. Share your professional story draft and story snippet with people whose opinions you trust. I know it may be tempting to share it with somebody who will tell you it's perfect (thanks, Mom!), but it's important to choose people who are going to be real with you. You want these pieces to sound like you, so lean on people who know you well enough to give you some honest feedback and make any necessary changes.

Rehearse and Share It

The goal here is for you to get super comfy with your professional story, and I want to be clear here because people operate differently.

If rehearsing your story word for word feels unnatural and robotic, ditch the script. Practice just the gist of the story rather than trying to memorize it. One thing that tripped me up when I first started speaking on stages was that I would practice my keynotes word for word, which was fine when I remembered it, but when somebody in the audience coughed or I felt the nerves getting out of control, I'd blank on what came next.

If you are similar and operate better with an outline or framework rather than a script, do that instead. The goal is for you to be confident when speaking, not to recite your story like you're reading from a teleprompter. This flexibility can actually make your storytelling more engaging and authentic.

Now, on the flip side, if you do better with a script, rock on. Trust me, if you don't already know which camp you fall into, you'll learn pretty quick.

In terms of rehearsal, again, this will be an individual preference. Some people like to recite while looking in the mirror; others like to record themselves speaking and then play it back. If you like to record yourself, you can pop your script into the speaker notes section of Keynote or PowerPoint and turn on rehearsal mode if you want to either record or time yourself.

If neither of those options work for you, employ a buddy with whom you feel comfortable and read it to them. Funny story, but when I first started recording videos, I would break out in nervous hives up to my earlobes. So when I was recording my first online course, I put a wig and glasses on my camera and called him Frank. Insane? Maybe, but it worked! Sometimes just taking things less seriously helps to lessen the anxiety.

So now that you've read through your story and rehearsed it, it's time to put it out into the world.

Revise as Needed

Look for smaller opportunities to practice your professional story with real-life humans and gauge their response. What resonated with them? Were there parts of your story that they seemed bored with?

Be curious rather than self-conscious, because refining and learning what works is going to set you up for future successes. Remember, the goal isn't perfection but connection.

Embrace this process of revision as an ongoing thing, not a one-time task. Your professional story will evolve as you do, and that's a good thing! It means you're growing, and your story should grow with you.

Remember: your personal brand isn't just a sneaky, salesy way of marketing yourself. It's about finding and sharing your story in a way that connects and resonates with others.

Each time you share your story, you're not just finding more professional opportunities; you're also fostering real connections that go beyond small talk. Your story is a beacon; it's time to let it shine.

The Psychology of Color

You're just about set in creating your magnetic personal brand for networking, but there's one piece that's still missing, one that despite all my practice networking *still* stumps me every time: what to wear!

Don't worry, this Lululemon-legging- and Costco-sweatshirt-wearing mom is nowhere near qualified to tell you how to dress, but what we should discuss is the psychology of color and how certain colors may affect the mood of those around you and even your own self-confidence.

Simply put, the psychology of color looks at how different colors influence behavior and mood. And while you may have heard about it in the context of web design and marketing, it's also important to consider how the colors that you wear could possibly affect the mood, feelings, and perceptions of those who you interact with.

The cool thing about color psychology is that it's not location dependent, meaning that no matter where you are in the world, many colors evoke the same emotions. A recent study done by Dr. Christine Mohr and Dr. Domicele Jonauskaite, who researched the universality of color-emotion associations across 30 countries, found that some universal color-emotion associations exist, with the exceptions being red (which symbolizes good luck in China) and purple (which symbolizes sadness in Greece).[7]

Here's how you can leverage the psychology of color in your wardrobe for your next networking event:

- Want to appear more confident and attract attention? Red can be a powerful color for situations where you want to appear bold and energetic. Some events red would work well in are public speaking engagements, meetings, or more formal events where you want to stand out in the crowd.
- Want to appear joyful and vibrant? Incorporating yellow into your outfit can give off positive vibes, ideal for creative environments, presentations, or job interviews.
- Want to give off sophisticated vibes? While black is linked to sadness, it's also associated with sophistication and class. I recently have been

wearing all black during speaking gigs to let the focus be more on my material, and it also conveys a more serious, professional tone. Black is a great option for any occasion, formal or informal, if it makes you feel stylish and cool.

- Want people around you to feel chill? Blue is associated with calmness, contentment, and relaxation, so it's a great choice for situations that feel more stressful. It's a universally liked color that tends to have a calming effect on both the wearer and those around them, so if you are feeling those nerves before a social event, reach for this color to ground yourself.
- Want to show that you're all about growth? Symbolizing progression, wearing green can signal growth and a forward-thinking attitude. It's a natural color that can put others at ease and invite more open conversations.

There isn't a universally "correct" color to wear, and people are unlikely to have extreme emotional reactions like bursting into tears over black attire or becoming angry at someone wearing red. The research on how specific colors influence our emotions is still in its early stages. Dr. Jonauskaite notes that while people may report associating certain colors with specific feelings – such as joy with yellow or envy with green – these associations are more about our mental perceptions than direct emotional experiences.

So, really, even though color psychology provides some interesting research showing that colors do affect you and those around you, it's less about the color you're rocking and more about what that color represents for you.

When you're picking out your outfit, think about the vibe you're aiming to send out into the world. If you're feeling like Beyoncé in your bright red pantsuit, chances are you'll radiate that same energy outward. Whether you're stepping into a networking gig, sitting down for a job interview, or just hanging out casually, choosing colors that align with how you want to be seen can be a game-changer. So go ahead, wear what makes you feel like the best version of yourself!

5 | Crafting Your Networking Game Plan

Setting Networking Goals That Work for You

Why did you pick up this book?

Maybe you're in the midst of a big life or career change, itching to start something new, or maybe you realize that flying solo has fewer perks than getting out there and growing your connections.

Or perhaps you're just ready to do the uncomfortable things you've been avoiding and see what happens, because YOLO, right?

Whatever your reasons, carving out some solid networking goals is your first step toward turning casual conversations into something more meaningful.

So what is your big "why"? If you haven't really considered it, take this moment right now to do so. One question that I like to ask my clients when they can't uncover their why is, "What would success look like for you?"

Imagine you're at a small reception after work at a local coffee shop. You leave the event feeling elated, having gotten exactly what you came for.

What happened at that event to make you feel so accomplished? Did you forge some deep connections beyond just swapping business cards? Learn about a new podcast or book, or pick up career tips from someone you respect? Perhaps you shared your knowledge and earned admiration from your peers, landed a meeting, or even a new client. Maybe, just maybe, you're proud because you faced your fears and proved to yourself that you could do it.

Reflecting on this topic, Phil Mershon, the Director of Experience for Social Media Examiner and author of *Unforgettable: The Art and Science of Creating Memorable Experiences*, shared an important story during our conversation that perfectly illustrates the power of intentional networking.[1]

He told me about a recent conference where attendees Amanda and Daniel dramatically changed their networking approach. Amanda, who used to attend sessions passively, set a new goal to prioritize networking over simply consuming content. This shift led her to actively participate in table talks, even running one herself, and staying engaged throughout. Similarly, Daniel, encouraged by his boss to overcome his social anxiety, took a proactive approach by attending and engaging in meetups well before the conference started.

Their proactive approaches not only transformed their own experiences but also inspired a ripple effect, encouraging others to step out of their comfort zones and engage more meaningfully too.

As you jot down your goals for the next networking event, think about the outcomes that feel most relevant to you. Getting crystal clear on what you're after isn't just about navigating the event with purpose; it's about recognizing your wins, whether they're handshake deals or simply getting better at small talk without the nausea and giving yourself a well-deserved pat on the back.

Identifying Your Networking Style

One thing that's been a total game-changer for me is shaking up the traditional idea of what networking is supposed to look like. Mention networking to anyone, and they'll probably paint a picture of those stand-around tables, a cheese platter somewhere in the background, and circles of people making small talk.

But trust me, there's a whole world of networking out there that goes way beyond those clichés!

At its core, networking is really just social interactions. It's about making connections, sharing interests, and building relationships. This realization opens up a whole new perspective: networking doesn't have to be a formal, stiff affair. Forget the forced smiles and elevator pitches at stuffy events. You can decide how and where you want to do it.

The beauty of networking lies in its versatility. It can accommodate so many different preferences and personalities. If you like more casual, laid-back vibes, a coffee chat or a walk in the park can be just as valuable for making connections as any professional mixer. Even if you're battling an extreme form of social anxiety like agoraphobia, digital platforms like LinkedIn offer another avenue, allowing for the exchange of ideas and collaborations across the globe, all from the comfort of your home. It doesn't have to be a ballroom or nothing!

Networking is about finding your squad: those individuals who resonate with your values, goals, and interests. When you start to view networking through this lens, I hope you'll find it easier to navigate and more – dare I say it – fun. By aligning your networking efforts with activities that reflect your genuine interests and preferred social settings, you make the process more enjoyable and effective, truly allowing your personality to shine through and attract like-minded professionals with more ease than you ever imagined.

Here's how to identify and rock your unique networking style.

Discover Your Personality Type

Often people mix up introversion with social anxiety, thinking they're one and the same. But actually, they're totally different things! According to Dr. Ellen Hendriksen, "While introversion/extroversion are about energy and stimulation, social anxiety is about fear – it's the worry that a perceived 'fatal flaw' will be revealed and judgment and rejection will follow."[2]

In other words, social anxiety is about fear or a perceived threat, whereas introversion is more about energy and how you recharge your social battery. However, knowing where you land on the introversion/extroversion spectrum is incredibly important for networking because you need to tailor your approach in a way that suits your unique needs.

According to the American Psychological Association, introversion is "orientation toward the internal private world of one's self and one's inner thoughts and feelings, rather than toward the outer world of people and things. Introversion is a broad personality trait and, like extraversion, exists on a continuum of attitudes and behaviors. Introverts are relatively more withdrawn, retiring, reserved, quiet, and deliberate; they may tend to mute or guard expressions of positive affect, adopt more skeptical views or positions, and prefer to work independently."[3]

So what does that mean in nonscientific speak? If you lean more introverted, you'll likely have a preference for more chill, laid-back atmospheres because loud ones are overstimulating. You also probably hit a clear point when socializing where you feel like you're ready to go home and rest. You recharge your social battery best alone, maybe tucked under a blanket with a little treat, scrolling through TikTok, or having a nap.

On the flip side, if you lean more extroverted, you're likely the life of the party, thriving on the buzz of a crowd and drawing energy from being around a bunch of people. It's like your social battery gets a turbo charge from interactions, and you can't get enough.

You can also fall somewhere in the middle between introversion and extroversion. This would make you an ambivert, which means somebody who is socially versatile. It can depend entirely on the day, the context, or your mood how you draw and spend energy. Some days, you build energy from being around others, thriving on interaction and the dynamic buzz of group settings. At other times you prefer the comfort of your favorite well-worn sweater, a podcast in your headphones, and quiet reflection. Ambiverts are versatile, adaptable, and can find comfort in both the spotlight and the shadows depending on the circumstances.

While social anxiety is associated more often with introversion, you can absolutely be socially anxious and also be an extrovert or ambivert. Here's what networking might typically look like based on your personality type.

If you're an introvert, you might feel overwhelmed just *thinking* about networking, especially in large group settings where you don't know anyone. The chatter of a crowded room can make you instantly overstimulated, where every cough or laugh sounds like it's coming through a megaphone. When you get to this point, where everything sounds like static on a TV, it can feel impossible to focus or find any sort of enjoyment in the moment. Most of your time is spent wondering why you decided to come and trying to figure out how to escape without anyone noticing.

If you are introverted, here are some strategies for networking with more ease:

1. **Set realistic expectations:** If you're introverted, you may have a shorter social battery life than extroverts. For me, my social battery is drained after approximately two hours, like clockwork, so I need to plan my outing accordingly. Not sure when your time limit is? Next time you're having a social interaction, set a timer. When you feel your energy level crashing, check your timer and write it down or make a mental note. This information is so valuable because now you can start to organize your most important networking activities within that time frame without feeling overextended and burnt out afterwards.

2. **Focus on meaningful conversations:** You don't need to enter a room with the goal to meet as many people as possible; focus instead on having one or a few deeper conversations, something that introverts feel more comfortable doing. You can do this by spending some time before an event researching who will be there and invest your precious energy focused on the select few people you're excited to meet. It may also be helpful to think of some interesting questions or topics that you'd like to discuss to help steer the conversation below the surface. We'll discuss conversation starters and navigating small talk in future chapters, but for now, consider having a general idea of what might be interesting to bring up. I always have a couple of interesting podcast episodes in the back of my mind that I'm ready to share.

3. **Schedule downtime:** After I speak on stage, I nap. I love being able to go back to my quiet hotel room and rest, but even without a hotel room, I get so tired after socializing that I will find any couch, chair, or surface to lay down on. If you are similar, and need time after an event to decompress and process your interactions, don't go to networking events where you're expected to be "on" afterward, like a networking breakfast where you head to work afterwards. Take the time that you need to recharge when your body is asking for it.

If you're extroverted but socially anxious, you may have a paradoxical emotional response to networking, because even though you're energized and excited by social interactions, you're also fearful of them. On one hand, you're drawn to social gatherings, feeling a natural pull toward meeting and interacting with people. However, when you arrive, you might feel a wave of panic wash over you.

"Why didn't I dress up more; everybody else is all done up! Do I look frumpy?"

"This person is so accomplished, there's no way I can start a conversation with them. I have nothing to offer."

Your fear of being judged or not living up to expectations can quickly dampen your excitement and sour your mood. You might also spend a lot of time after the event worried that you didn't leave the right impression or ruminating about all the mistakes that you made during your interactions.

If you're an extrovert with social anxiety, here are some networking strategies to help you shine:

1. **Don't let your emotions run the show:** When I was battling agoraphobia, the one thing that kept me trapped in my house was letting how I felt dictate my actions. I felt scared by the idea of leaving my house, and that feeling felt like a fact. *I am scared, so this action I'm considering must be dangerous.* It wasn't until I was able to separate how I feel from what is real that I was able to thrive in social settings.

   If you are an extrovert with social anxiety, instead of focusing on every single thing that could go wrong, think about what might go right. Imagine yourself leaving the event, getting into your car or back home, feeling energized, inspired, connected. Just like it can be a slog getting to the gym but feels great after a good sweaty workout, you were wired to do this thing that feels scary.

2. **Channel your energy:** Extroverts are born with the natural gift of gab, and yet when you're battling social anxiety at social events, it can be hard to remember your core strengths that lie beneath the surface of nerves.

   One way to take what your mama gave you and put it to good use is to focus your energy by setting some clear networking goals for yourself. Pick a number of people who you want to approach, or those who you want to get to know on a deeper level. Rather than trying to do it all and be a networking master, siphon that energy into goals that feel important to you.

It might also be helpful to figure out where your anxiety is triggered. For some, it's introducing yourself to strangers; for others it's figuring out how to end a conversation, or maybe it's trying to figure out what to do when you hit an awkward silence. Knowing specifically what makes you feel social anxiety can be helpful to overcome it by preparing yourself with conversation starters and learning how to exit a conversation gracefully. We'll get into both in later chapters.

If you're a socially anxious ambivert, you're like the twist cone of personality types, a swirl of craving the buzz of social interaction combined with seeking the peace of alone time. This can also be a challenge when it comes to networking because you need to find that perfect balance between socialization and solitude. You might find yourself pumped to head to a social event, and have no problem introducing yourself to the first person you see standing nearest you. But then you find yourself in an awkward surface-level conversation about the weather with a person who keeps offering one-word answers and that quickly zaps all your energy. You excuse yourself to the washroom to regroup, and make some polite chitchat by the sink with a colleague before calling an Uber home.

Here are some networking tips for schmoozing as a socially anxious ambivert:

1. **Identify your peaks and valleys:** As an ambivert, there are times when you're ready to paaaartay, and other times when you don't even want your pets to look at you. Pay attention to your pattern and schedule social events at the times when you're feeling it most. This will help you to use your extroverted side to your advantage.

    This might be particularly helpful for those who menstruate. According to a study done with 100 Polish women, the women got a spike in the urge to connect and mingle during the luteal phase, which rolls out right after ovulation and before the period kicks in.[4] This phase could naturally nudge ambiverts to lean into their extroverted side, making it a perfect example of how social interactions rely on both biology and learned behaviors.

2. **Be gentle on yourself:** One of the challenges for ambiverts is feeling like your ability to socialize changes constantly. Some days, you

may find yourself as the life of the party, others, small talk may feel like a root canal. That's okay. If you feel more socially anxious one day, you aren't taking a step back; it's ingrained in who you are. Be kind to yourself before, during, and after networking events. Remember, every interaction is a learning opportunity, not a test that you can fail or ace. Meditation and self-care will go a long way in your networking journey.

Still not sure which personality type belongs to you? Here's a quiz created by Dr. Adam Grant, a renowned organizational psychologist, author, and professor at the Wharton School at the University of Pennsylvania that can help you figure it out. The answer may be your gateway to personal insight, growth, and more meaningful social interactions: https://ideas.ted.com/quiz-are-you-an-extrovert-introvert-or-ambivert.[5]

No matter what your personality type – introvert, extrovert, or ambivert – navigating social interactions with social anxiety can be a challenge. But that doesn't mean that you're destined for a life of dodging events where other people may be hanging out. The key here is to figure out which personality type you fall into, and then find opportunities to connect that feel manageable and true to you. It's about craving your own networking path that respects both your challenges and your capabilities.

So let's get to the fun part: finding those golden opportunities where you'll shine instead of living in the shadow of others.

Finding Events and Experiences That Align with Your Comfort Level

I've seen it time and again – socially anxious professionals, myself included, trying to squeeze into the traditional networking mold.

It never felt right.

Every time I'd leave a networking event, I'd beat myself up for not radiating confidence or mingling with ease. But then it clicked – I didn't need to change who I was to fit the networking scene. Instead, I started finding ways to network that felt natural for me. Suddenly, networking shifted from a dreaded task to something that genuinely felt rewarding and fulfilling.

Once I embraced this more diverse approach to networking, I began to see opportunities everywhere, not just in the crowded rooms of formal events but in coffee shops, on LinkedIn, on Zoom calls, and casual lunch meetups and daytime activities. Here, I could engage in deeper, more meaningful conversations, rather than just trying to hand out as many business cards as possible.

The key to successful networking lies in finding events and experiences that align with your unique comfort level. Even though it may still feel uncomfortable at first, seeking out opportunities that fit your personal style will allow you to engage in a way that feels far more natural and less performative.

Let's jump into how to find those events and experiences that align better with who you are, one baby step at a time:

Track Your Comfort Levels in a Networking Journal

Think of tracking your networking comfort like keeping a food diary, but instead of counting calories or trying to determine intolerances or allergies, you're measuring your social battery! Next time you have a social event, even if it's a one-on-one interaction, grab a notebook or open a new note on your smartphone.

Document the vibe of each place, the number of people included, and how the interactions made you feel. Was it an energy booster or a complete drain? Which conversations left you feeling at ease and content, and which ones had you plotting the nearest escape route or checking your phone constantly?

Here's an example of a networking journal entry:

Date: 15 April 2024
Event Name: Women in Business Breakfast
Event Type: Small event, roughly 20 women, seated with buffet options. There was also a speaker on contract negotiations.
Location: The Orchard Room, Maple Grove Boutique Hotel, Vancouver
Objective of Attending: To meet at least one new professional woman in my local area to discuss the unique challenges involved with entrepreneurship and support each other, and also to learn more about contract negotiations, something that I struggle with.

Preparation: Mindset and mediation practice, researched the speaker and location, looked at who else was attending on the LinkedIn event page.

Person/People Met: Elena Martinez

Contact Info: elena.martinez@innovatebiz.com

Key Details: Director of Strategic Initiatives at InnovateBiz Solutions. Potential for collaboration on a new tech startup focused on enhancing digital marketing tools for small businesses, or training workshops for employees.

Conversation Highlights: Both interested in the role of AI in marketing, both live in the same neighborhood and have kids around the same age. Both love reality television and had a long conversation about the latest season of *Vanderpump Rules*.

Follow-Up Actions: Send a thank you email and follow up with a connection request on LinkedIn

Comfort Level: 7

I felt more comfortable sitting down and talking at the table than I did trying to make chitchat standing in line at the buffet. The venue was small and there weren't many people there, so it made diving into conversation feel easier. The noise level was pretty low so I didn't feel overstimulated. The only time I felt uncomfortable was when we hit an awkward silence, but then the speaker came on stage so it was an easy way to break from the conversation. Overall, it wasn't too painful.

Personal Insights: I learned that I prefer networking while seated. There's something about standing around that feels really formal and makes me feel like I'm performing. Sitting helps me feel more grounded.

Overall Reflection: It was okay. I made one contact, which was my goal, and I learned something new. I like events early in the day like that because my energy wasn't already spent from interacting with coworkers all day. I would maybe do it again.

Mood Tracker: Satisfied. It wasn't life changing but not ruminating too much post event.

Additional Notes: Knowing the parking layout beforehand was really helpful because I knew what to expect.

Over time, you'll see patterns in your networking journal, and patterns equal power. The knowledge you gain will show you where you shine and what to skip. It's all about playing to your strengths without forcing yourself into situations that just aren't you.

Scout for Social Spaces That Feel Safe

Now that you've gotten a better understanding of what feels okay and what doesn't for you, it's time to find events and experiences that fit your unique comfiness level. This doesn't mean settling for less; it means targeting more of what truly works for you. As a no fear networker, you want to select environments where you can thrive, not just survive!

Here is a nonexhaustive list of environments to consider as you build your networking schedule. Since we're thinking of networking as a muscle that we need to exercise, I've divided each into "low-impact," "medium-intensity," or "high-intensity" activities:

"Low-Impact" Networking Options   These options are all about easing into connections without the pressure cooker environment. You're looking at laid-back interactions where the setting is just as comforting as your favorite coffee shop corner. Whether it's a digital hangout where you can contribute when you feel it, or a casual meetup with just a few folks, these environments are designed to keep the stress levels low and the approachability high. Perfect for anyone who wants to network but isn't quite ready for a higher-stakes, high-stimulation environment yet.

Online Forums and Communities   If you want to dip your toes into networking without diving headfirst into live interactions, online forums and communities are a great place to start. You can take your time to think of a response, come and go as you please, and you don't have to worry about body language.

Another perk is choosing conversations where you know you can contribute. The hardest part of in-person conversations is finding common interests, but online communities are categorized, taking out the guesswork. While online communities might not replace in-person networking, they're a great way to build confidence and maybe even meet people you'll chat with offline!

Some fun places to hang out in online communities are Reddit for various topics, Quora for Q&A on almost any subject, LinkedIn or Facebook groups for career interests, and Instagram group chats for mutual interests.

Zoom Chats   If face-to-face meetings still make your palms sweat, Zoom chats are a good baby step. You can meet someone from your couch or favorite cozy chair, which feels more grounding. If you need a break, just turn off your camera and jump back in when you're ready. Plus, you can glance at notes on your phone or computer for questions or topics.

Feeling your social battery draining? Just close your laptop and blame it on a weak internet connection…kidding (sort of)! Having a predetermined end time is also great if you struggle with exiting conversations.

Virtual Webinars and Workshops   These are great because they offer a safe space to engage with industry leaders and peers without crowding into a cramped space. They're a low-pressure way to build your network and learn something new simultaneously.

To build your networking stamina, choose ones with interactive elements like live polls, Q&A sessions, or breakout rooms. Treat a webinar like an online meeting: draft questions, research the speaker, and follow up on LinkedIn or email after the event.

Interest-Based Clubs   Networking can be easier when there's already common ground, whether business or personal. If breaking the ice is your biggest challenge, interest-based clubs do the legwork for you! Conversations here feel more meaningful.

Interest-based clubs are ongoing, like a book club that meets monthly, allowing you to build rapport over time. They also feel lower pressure because you aren't joining just to network, unlike more formal settings.

Peer Mentoring Circles   If you want to step up your networking game in a smaller group setting, peer mentoring circles focus on mutual growth and support. I joined one for entrepreneurs and found it helpful and supportive, not nearly as intimidating as traditional networking events. Members give and receive advice and share current challenges.

For example, a small group of women in digital marketing catch up on Zoom every couple of weeks, discussing industry trends and sharing tips.

One member acts as a facilitator to keep the conversation focused and organized.

Overall, these circles offer a structured yet flexible environment to enhance your networking abilities and foster professional relationships.

Coworking Spaces   If you work remotely, networking can be challenging with only a snoring dog or purring cat for company. Shake things up by renting a desk at a coworking space.

Imagine popping into a shared workspace instead of a stiff corporate office. You can choose to be there when you're feeling up to it, avoiding forced socializing.

In a coworking space, you might grab coffee with a startup founder or join a casual lunch on the terrace. These spontaneous interactions can ease nerves. The diverse mix of people from different fields can enrich your network, making connections feel more natural and less transactional.

Farmers Markets   Plot twist! Networking doesn't have to be in a boardroom; you can do it at your local farmers market while browsing fresh produce, artisan breads, and homemade jams. These markets invite casual, friendly interactions. Chat with local farmers about their business, swap recipes, or learn about craft vendors. Farmers markets often serve as community hubs, creating a warm, welcoming environment that feels less intimidating.

I once met a fellow Carleton University alum at a farmers market in Oahu, Hawaii. This spontaneous connection led to a great conversation and an extra bag of Kona coffee beans. Farmers markets are perfect for low-impact networking like that.

Group Fitness Classes   Group fitness classes are great for networking if you have social anxiety. They incorporate "parallel play," where you engage in activities near others without forced interaction. You're focused on your workout, not small talk, but as you keep showing up, you might help someone put away their gear or share a laugh after a tough session. Physical activity also boosts endorphins, making you feel more relaxed and open to connections.

Dog Parks   Dog parks are excellent for networking with social anxiety because they provide a natural icebreaker – your dog! The atmosphere is relaxed, and the focus is on the animals. Make an effort to strike up conversations, whether it's a friendly hello or asking which dog belongs to whom. Dog parks often become regular hangout spots, so you'll see familiar faces, making interactions easier and more meaningful over time.

Community Garden   No pets? No problem! A community garden is a great way to enjoy the sunshine and exercise your networking muscle. You're planting seeds for potential friendships and professional connections. This setting strips away the formalities of typical networking events, allowing for casual conversations over gardening. You'll see familiar faces regularly, which helps build rapport. Sitting down or being low to the ground can also be calming. The sense of shared purpose and teamwork fosters bonding.

Place of Worship   If you're part of a faith community, your place of worship can be a perfect spot to build meaningful professional connections in a low-pressure environment. My husband and daughter have Indigenous roots, and we connected with an Indigenous priest in Ottawa for our daughter's baptism. This led to regular attendance at an Indigenous mass, where we met many wonderful people.

Faith communities provide common ground, with shared beliefs and values, making social interactions feel less intimidating. The established trust and goodwill make it easier to open up. Spend extra time before or after services to meet people, and look for opportunities to connect outside, like volunteering for events or joining small group meetups.

Public Transportation and Traveling   When I asked my community to share the craziest places they've networked, many mentioned serendipitous experiences on public transportation or while traveling. It might not seem like a networking goldmine, but some of the best connections are made there.

Recently, I was waiting for a delayed flight and ran into an old coworker. We caught up about work and travel, turning wasted time into a valuable connection. Others shared similar stories, like landing a private coaching client from an Uber ride or finding a job opportunity while chatting on a subway bench.

Being in the same place at the same time naturally sparks conversation. It's not always stress-free, and introverts might find it draining, but the "we're in this together" vibe often makes it easier to open up. For some, traveling to new places can even ease social anxiety.

I joke that there are two versions of me: Ottawa Mick and Travel Mick. Away from home, I'm more outgoing because I know I'll likely never see these people again. You never know who you might run into – one minute it's a CEO, the next a local artist.

To make the most of traveling or public transportation for networking, stay approachable. Resist the urge to plug in your headphones. Look for people with open body language to chat with. A little compliment or small talk can lead to surprising conversations and boost your confidence.

In Lineups Believe it or not, those lineups where you shuffle your feet and check the time on your phone? It's the perfect chance to try and strike up a quick conversation.

Whether you're lined up at your favorite coffee spot, waiting to check out at a retail store, or inching forward in a concert line, every minute is a golden opportunity to chat up someone new.

Sparking a conversation in a lineup can feel less intimidating for somebody with social anxiety because it's generally in a more casual setting, the line is moving along so you don't have to worry about ending the conversation, and you have something to break the ice – whatever you're in line waiting for! Consider this.

> You're in line at your favorite bakery on a busy Saturday morning. It's the kind of place where the croissants are worth the hype and the coffee is strong enough to spark any conversation. You notice the person in front of you is wearing a T-shirt from a concert that you attended last weekend. Here's your in – just a quick mention of the event could open the door to a connection over shared love of classic rock.

So the next time you're in line, resist the urge to compulsively check your phone and instead take a look around. A friendly comment, smile, or a compliment could be the start of your next meaningful interaction. Remember, networking sometimes just starts with a grin and saying, "So, not the fastest line today, huh?" (or eh if you're Canadian).

Public Lectures and Talks These events are not just about learning but also about connecting with like-minded people. Since everyone shares a common interest, it's a great low-impact networking option. Instead of sneaking out after the event, strike up a conversation with someone nearby or introduce yourself. Reach out to the speaker to thank them, ask a question, or share your favorite takeaway. When I speak at events, I appreciate LinkedIn connection requests with personalized notes and shared photos from the talk.

Walking Groups   Combining networking with movement can make conversations feel less intimidating. Walking side by side feels more like chatting with a friend and can ease anxiety. Next time you hear about a local walking group, lace up your sneakers and join in. You might make valuable connections while enjoying a nice workout.

Sports Teams   Why not mix a bit of fun with your networking efforts? Joining a sports team lets you stretch those networking muscles in an energizing environment.

The sense of teamwork and camaraderie extends beyond the field, making social interactions feel less daunting. Many teams also gather for a bite or drink after games, providing relaxed settings to connect on a personal level. Sports teams are diverse, pulling in people from all walks of life, broadening your network and perspectives. Whether it's soccer, basketball, or bowling, sports teams are a great way to network and create memorable connections.

"Medium-Intensity" Networking Options   Stepping it up a notch, medium-intensity networking is where you start to blend the casual with the strategic. It's for when you're ready to push your comfort zone just a little bit but aren't quite diving into the deep end yet. These environments typically balance structured activities with the freedom to mingle, making them ideal for those who want a bit more from their networking but still appreciate a safety net. Think of events like small industry trade shows or a group dinner where the crowds are manageable but the potential is significant. It's about finding that sweet spot between relaxed chats and goal-oriented networking.

Trade Shows   Trade shows can seem overwhelming, but they're great for medium-intensity networking because they offer structure and clear navigation. With a map and organized booths, you're not just wandering aimlessly.

Each booth offers an opportunity for "mini conversations," helping you practice introductions and exits. Awkward moments? Absolutely. But each one is a learning experience. You laugh it off, try again, and gain confidence with each interaction.

Don't go it alone! Bring a colleague or friend. It makes the experience more fun, less stressful, and gives you an escape plan if needed.

Breakfast Networking Groups Alright, let's be real – I'm not exactly the "up with the sun" type. In fact, I'm much more of a "zombie before caffeine" kind of gal. But hear me out; these early morning networking groups might just make a morning person out of you – or at least get you to set that early alarm.

These breakfast clubs are a gem for those who find big, bustling networking events overwhelming. They offer a calm oasis where you can tackle networking early while sipping on that much-needed coffee. Plus, they're usually a seated affair, which is perfect if you're more at ease chatting while sitting down.

If you can face the morning, or are already an early riser, these gatherings can be fruitful. They're about building and nurturing relationships over time, not just exchanging business cards. Who knows? Joining a breakfast club might not only expand your network but also become an important part of your morning ritual.

Panel Discussions and Q&A Sessions This one might feel like a stretch for those with performance anxiety, but isn't that what we're here for?! To stretch beyond your comfort zone? Panel discussions and Q&A sessions can be a game-changer for someone with social anxiety, especially if you're one of the speakers.

Here's why: the spotlight isn't all on you. Unlike a solo talk, you're sharing the stage with several people, so the focus is spread around. It's a great way to ease into presenting and get used to the adrenaline rush, but with the ability to pass the mic if it feels too much.

The sessions follow an agenda, offering predictability, which helps with social anxiety. You can prepare and rehearse, especially if you know the questions in advance. I find panel discussions less stressful than off-stage conversations due to the structured format and the ability to pause. While others speak, you get time to think about what to add or pass on a question if needed.

So if you've been avoiding speaking opportunities because of social anxiety, a panel discussion might be just what you need. You might enjoy it more than you imagined!

Professional Development Workshops   Workshops, especially interactive ones, are perfect for developing skills and leveling up your networking game. They focus on big ideas, making conversations flow more easily.

Workshops span hours to days, giving you time to warm up and interact at your own pace. They encourage idea swapping and brainstorming, fostering meaningful connections.

Interactive workshops are ideal for active participation and immediate application of what you learn. If small talk makes you cringe, this is the perfect networking option for building lasting relationships.

Casual Business Lunches or Coffee   Sitting down with a coffee or meal in a familiar spot makes networking feel more relaxed and manageable. Picking a local place you know well can help you focus on the conversation instead of worrying about logistics.

Seated conversations tend to be more personal and in-depth, which is easier for those with social anxiety. If you prefer unstructured networking, the flexible nature of lunch or coffee meetups is ideal. With no set end time, you control how long you engage and when to leave.

Small Group Dinners   One of my favorite ways to network is at small group dinners. I remember my first invite to an entrepreneurs' dinner at a sushi restaurant. Normally, I'd make a million excuses, but my friend was so outgoing and made everyone feel at ease, so I decided to go.

The setup was perfect: circular tables, dimmed lights, and a warm welcome with introductions. Conversations flowed seamlessly, and I had so much fun that I haven't missed an invite since. I still chat with people I met at those events years later.

With fewer attendees, conversations are more focused and meaningful, especially with a great host. Starting with a common connection and discussing shared challenges makes it easier to connect on a deeper level. This kind of depth is hard to achieve in bigger, noisier settings.

Small group dinners also offer a controlled environment. Knowing who will attend in advance is gold. You can look up attendees' LinkedIn profiles or ask the host for info and prep conversation starters. This can make a huge difference if social anxiety hits.

"High-Intensity" Networking Options   Ready to turn it up to 11? You got this! High-intensity networking is for those who want to make the most out of every handshake and business card exchange. These are high-energy, often larger-scale events where making connections is the main focus. From bustling conferences to formal networking dinners, these settings are designed to maximize interaction and open as many doors as possible in a short time. They're perfect for the socially anxious professional who is eager to dive into the thick of things, armed with a stack of business cards and a polished pitch to boot.

Industry Conferences   Stepping into an industry conference might feel intimidating, especially if large social gatherings aren't really your jam. But here's the thing: these conferences are more than just hustle and bustle and free pens; they offer a huge opportunity to maximize the time that you spend networking and meeting lots of cool people at once.

Think of each session as a small step. You're surrounded by people who are probably just as hopeful (and maybe just as nervous or more!) as you are to make meaningful connections. And here's a little secret: many of them are looking for someone exactly like you to exchange ideas with. You're not alone in feeling a bit out of your element, but you can take control of your itinerary to make it feel as comfortable as possible.

If you feel more at ease chatting up the person next to you at a session, fill up your calendar with them. If you know that you'll shine more during lunch and/or networking parties, save your energy for those and catch the session replays later. One of the worst mistakes I made early on as a speaker at conferences was that I ignored my networking preferences. My calendar was jam-packed with events and sessions because I didn't want to waste any opportunity that I had. But it left me feeling drained and miserable, and sometimes dreading the next session or meetup.

It wasn't until I got more intentional about picking and choosing what I attended based on what truly suited me that I started to enjoy these events more. By focusing on quality over quantity, I was able to engage more deeply with the people I met and get more out of each interaction. This approach not only made the whole experience more fulfilling, but it also helped me conserve my energy for the activities where I could really shine. So tailor your conference agenda around what matters most and feels best to you.

Also, don't be afraid to take breaks. It's important to give yourself permission to step back and recharge when you need to. Find a quiet corner to regroup, step outside for a breath of fresh air, or even skip a session to relax in your hotel room. (I love taking an afternoon nap during conferences when possible.) Remember, you don't have to be "on" all the time to make the most of a conference.

Speed Networking Events   Speed networking events are like the espresso shot of social interactions – quick and intense. Think of it as a HIIT workout (high-intensity interval training) for networking: you have just a few minutes to make an impression before moving to the next person. It's high pressure but offers a chance to perfect your pitch. If a conversation gets awkward, a buzzer rescues you, so no need for creative exit strategies.

These events are about rapid exposure to social interactions, fitting the "flooding" exposure therapy category, where you face your fears head-on. Everyone is there to learn and improve, not to judge. Prepare your intro, listen actively, and have your business cards or LinkedIn ready to connect further. If it gets too much, it's okay to step out and take a breath.

This approach may seem daunting, but it could be exactly what you need to overcome social anxieties. You might even enjoy the challenge and surprise yourself with how much you can handle!

Public Speaking Engagements   Imagine stepping onto a stage, your heart pounding and palms sweating, feeling like you're about to jump out of an airplane without a parachute. That was me every time I grabbed the mic, but believe it or not, public speaking eventually became my secret weapon against social anxiety.

In the beginning, the adrenaline rush was intense, my hands felt numb, my heart raced. But surprisingly, each time I spoke, those overwhelming sensations started to fade faster. It was as if my body learned that the stage wasn't a threat to my survival, despite feeling exposed and scrutinized. Ann Handley, a powerhouse in professional speaking, bestselling author of

Everybody Writes: Your Go-To Guide for Creating Ridiculously Good Content, and someone whom I admire greatly, gets this. She says, "Standing on a stage alone is terrifying. We're unprotected, open to scrutiny, tapping into that ancient fear of being cast out from the tribe."[6]

Ann offers some game-changing advice that I took to heart: ditch the lectern and move closer to your audience, making the space less about barriers and more about connection. She says, "Bridge the gap by standing as close to the edge of the stage as you can, getting physically closer to your audience." This small shift helped me see the crowd not as judges, but as a community cheering for my success.

And when it comes to feedback? Ann advises focusing on what genuinely helps you grow. "Pay attention to what's useful. You will have a hater – it's just part of being vulnerable and putting yourself out there. If everyone loves what you're doing, maybe you're not pushing enough boundaries." This perspective was a lifeline for me, reminding me that real growth comes from stepping out of comfort zones and sometimes facing criticism.

Every speech became a step toward regaining control over my anxiety, turning nerve-wracking experiences into opportunities for growth. I used every applause and nod as fuel, building my confidence not just on stage, but in every area of my life where anxiety once controlled me.

Adding to this, my friend Melanie Deziel, top-rated keynote speaker and author of *The Content Fuel Framework* and *Prove It: Exactly How Modern Marketers Earn Trust*, opened up about her own struggles during and after a huge conference we were both speaking at.

Despite rocking the stage, the networking bits that come after are a different beast for her, thanks to her autism. She shared, "When I'm on stage... my role is clear. Everybody else's role is clear. Like...everybody knows what their role is in that environment. When I'm at a networking hall...it's way more open. I don't know what the expectations are...it's just a lot more."[7]

Melanie's honesty highlights an important truth: sometimes, the spotlight can actually feel safer than the crowd. Environments can affect you in many unexpected ways, and your strengths can shine in one setting and feel tested in another, so don't write off speaking engagements until you give them a try.

VIP Receptions   VIP receptions are often smaller and more exclusive, and that's exactly why they're great for anyone wrestling with social anxiety.

Even though the pressure may feel higher because of the power statuses of the people in attendance, the smaller crowd means more meaningful interactions and less noise to compete with. And because these receptions are often tied to specific interests or industries, you already have something in common with everyone there.

The one event that I always go to during conferences is the speakers' party. It's like having a built-in conversation cheat sheet where I know I can go up to anybody and ask what their talk is about rather than simply what they do for a living. This usually opens the gateway to deeper conversations because people get a chance to talk about what they're passionate about, not just where they work. Passion is contagious, and I always find myself loosening up when people are excitedly chatting about something.

So there you have it, some low-impact, medium-intensity, and high-intensity networking options to start exercising your networking muscle. And the truth is, this list only scratches the surface of where you can network, because meaningful conversations can happen anywhere if you're open to them.

Remember, when it comes to networking with social anxiety, you make the rules. Never feel pressured to stick only to high-intensity situations if they don't mesh with your vibe. It's totally okay to mix it up based on what feels right at the moment, or decide that one intensity or networking environment works better for you. You're in charge, not your social anxiety or societal pressures to conform to just one networking box.

Redefine What Networking Looks Like for You

At this point, you've probably realized that there's no set playbook for networking. It's all up to you: when you network, where it happens, and how you go about it. This is about crafting your own unique approach to connecting with others, in ways that feel right to you.

True networking doesn't require a formal setting, suit and tie, or shoes that leave you with blisters. In reality, some of the best networking can happen over coffee, at your kid's karate lesson, or even in the TSA line.

You also don't need to chase more. A small group dinner can be just as beneficial as a massive conference. Try not to focus solely on the numbers, and more on which environments you're most likely to bring your best self.

And lastly, and perhaps most importantly, networking doesn't have to feel icky.

As you start to attend more events and chat with people, you may also notice that sometimes you leave feeling energized and uplifted and other times you feel drained. Beyond your preferences, this difference often stems from the *type* of networking you're engaging in.

According to a study called "The Contaminating Effects of Building Instrumental Ties: How Networking Can Make Us Feel Dirty," there are essentially two kinds of networking: spontaneous and instrumental.[8] Instrumental networking is defined in the study as "a form of networking driven by specific, strategic goals typically related to professional advancement." This is the type you turn to when you're looking to climb the career ladder, or land that dream job or promotion. This networking style is very much intentional; you're essentially mapping out who you need to connect with to get what you need. While it's super effective for achieving specific career goals, it can feel a bit transactional or even make you feel a tad uncomfortable, because the connections are mainly for your own benefit.

One interesting observation from my interviews for this book is how people's body language shifts when the topic of instrumental networking comes up. Some frown, others grimace, and a few even shudder or shake their heads. Their voices often drop too, taking on a quieter tone, almost as if we're discussing something taboo or slightly off-putting.

Why is this? There's something about instrumental networking that just feels a bit dirty to many. Networking with a "what's in it for me?" attitude feels selfish. This really clashes with the idea of building genuine, give-and-take relationships that feel good. You want to believe positive things about yourself; that you are generous, altruistic, and community-oriented. Instrumental networking challenges these self-perceptions, forcing you to confront a more self-serving side that can seem at odds with your ideal self-image.

It's no surprise then that many find this approach uncomfy, preferring instead to engage in networking that allows them to maintain a sense of integrity and positive identity.

That brings us over to the other side of the networking coin: spontaneous networking. It's a whole different vibe compared to instrumental networking. Whenever I chat with those same people about their spontaneous networking moments, you can hear the excitement in their voice – they light up, their smiles are contagious, and they just can't wait to share all the details of those unexpected encounters.

Spontaneous networking is way more laid back. It happens serendipitously, no plans, no agendas. You might strike up a conversation at a party, or chat with someone in the washroom at a hockey game. There's none of that guilt you might get from instrumental networking, since you're not aiming to get something out of it, but if it happens, great!

To be clear, I don't think instrumental networking is bad and spontaneous networking is good. Both styles of networking have their value and place. But some people, especially those who are especially empathetic, get hung up on the idea that networking is purely instrumental. It's not all about the grind, meeting the "right" people, and filling up those contact lists for personal gain – that simply isn't the full picture.

So if you're one of those people who has a "dirty" perception of networking, I encourage you to challenge that perception by exploring more opportunities for spontaneous networking at more laid-back environments, like some of the low-impact options we discussed earlier.

In fact, don't even use the word "networking" as you plan your agenda. Just think of it as simply hanging out and getting to know new faces. Dive into chats without any big agendas. Share what you love, listen with genuine curiosity, and just let things flow naturally. You might find yourself amazed at how these kinds of interactions aren't just awesome for your career, but, surprisingly, they can also make you feel good about yourself.

Networking Skills for the Socially Anxious Professional

6 | Mastering the S-Word (Small Talk)

Small talk: just the phrase alone can send any socially anxious professional into a frenzy, furiously tapping away at their phone calculator, hoping to look engaged while secretly wishing for teleportation abilities to the nearest washroom stall for a quick escape.

Here's what small talk may look like in your mind, according to a funny TikTok by user Jeremy Andrew Davis[1]:

Speaker 1 Canned greeting.

Speaker 2 Repeated greeting.

Speaker 1 I have a name.

Speaker 2 I have a name too, but I'm not gonna remember yours cuz I'm concentrating too much on not coming across weird.

Speaker 1 Yeah, same here.

Speaker 2 Hey, the weather is, uh, really weathering.

Speaker 1 Yeah, we'll probably have more weather, the weather's tomorrow too.

Speaker 2 Sure, sure. Yeah, no weather quite weather's like the weather we have in this area.

Speaker 1 (obligatory chuckle) True.

For many of us, small talk feels daunting, uncomfortable, and frankly a bit painful. Yet it's also the bridge to meaningful conversations and connections with those around us.

In this section, we're diving headfirst into the world of small talk. We'll unpack what it really is, explain why it's not just idle chitchat, and arm you with some creative strategies to master it. Get ready to transform dreaded conversations about weather predictions and traffic commentary into engaging discussions!

Small talk, as defined by the *Oxford English Dictionary*, is "Polite conversation about unimportant or uncontroversial matters, especially as engaged in on social occasions."[2] Yet despite its seemingly superficial nature, there's more to small talk than just a way to fill awkward silences.

A Princeton University study done with ring-tailed lemurs found that social primates use specific sounds to communicate, but they're very picky about who they "talk to." As explained by coauthor Ipek Kulahci[3]:

> "By exchanging vocalizations, the animals are reinforcing their social bonds even when they are away from each other," Kulahci said. "This social selectivity in vocalizations is almost equivalent to how we humans keep in regular touch with our close friends and families, but not with everyone we know."

The study suggests that just as lemurs "chat" to feel close to their group members, humans engage in small talk for similar reasons. It's not just about passing time or filling silence; it's about reinforcing our connections with those around us. This study challenges the existing theories of language evolution that suggest that talking resulted from an increasing group size.

"As group size increased, grooming to form social bonds became too time consuming, so speech developed to save time while still expressing familiarity," explained Asif Ghazanfar, a professor of psychology and the Princeton Neuroscience Institute. But according to the lemur study, even when the group numbers increased, the vocalizations did not. The Princeton study shows that even casual conversation serves as an evolutionary mechanism for creating bonds, according to Ghazanfar:

> "Talking is a social lubricant, not necessarily done to convey information, but to establish familiarity...these vocalizations are equivalent to

> the chitchat that we do. People think that conversations are like exchanging mini-lectures full of information. But most of the time we have conversations and forget them when we're done because they're performing a purely social function."

Small talk, it seems, is not just an unavoidable formality in conversation, but an age-old practice of building and reinforcing social bonds, just like our primate cousins. But why does it seem so much easier for monkeys and lemurs to tolerate and nail it?

There are essentially two reasons why people have an aversion to small talk: either you find it to be a waste of time, or you aren't very good at it. I can thoroughly relate to both, and maybe you can too. Let's start by tackling the belief that small talk is a waste of time.

Here's an analogy that helped me rethink how I felt about small talk: Imagine language as a two-lane road. On the left fast lane of the highway, we're zooming with "imparting information," where it's all about the transfer of cold, hard facts and insights. Think of it as a delivery truck loaded up with boxes of knowledge, making its way from your brain warehouse to someone else's. This lane is where big ideas are exchanged from one person to the next.

Now imagine that there's a scenic route, the "phatic communication" lane. This isn't about delivering goods; it's like going for a slow ride on a sunny Sunday afternoon. It's the friendly honk as you pass by, the wave out the window to a neighbor, or the shared moment of laughter at a street corner. This communication doesn't necessarily teach us anything new about the world, but it teaches us about each other, fostering a sense of belonging and togetherness.

Both lanes on this road are crucial for building and maintaining relationships. The "imparting information" lane expands our minds, while the "phatic communication" lane brings us together.

Now let's go back to small talk. If we deconstruct it to its elements, small talk is really just language whose purpose is to build bridges between people. Doesn't that make you feel just a little bit guilty for the bad rep that it gets?

If you're still not convinced about the value and benefits of asking Mike how his weekend was, here are some more benefits of small talk. The more social interactions we have, the happier we feel. Although you might be rolling your eyes right now in disbelief that your commute and office niceties could actually be a positive thing, it's true. In a study involving 578 people in the United States and reported in PNAS (Proceedings of the National Academy of Sciences), researchers asked participants how happy they felt over the past 24 hours and where they stood on a "life satisfaction ladder" from 0 (worst possible life) to 10 (best possible life).[4]

People also shared details about their social interactions from the previous day. The study found that the more social interactions people had, the happier they reported being.

Think back to the beginning of the pandemic. As a socially anxious professional, I found that something interesting happened that changed my mindset around small talk completely. When everything shut down in March 2020, although I was worried about finances and what was going to happen next, I felt like social distancing was paradise for somebody like me who feels safest in isolation.

The first couple of weeks were bliss. I worked out, I made banana bread, I even made TikToks about how fun it was to be stuck in the house. Then, about two weeks into quarantine, something shifted. The short-term feelings of safety were disappearing, replaced by an increased sense of dread, panic, and depression fatigue.

Suddenly, I found myself idling a little longer at the window of the drive-thru, chatting just a bit longer on Zoom calls, waving from a distance to neighbors with whom I hadn't interacted often in the past.

In short, I found myself missing the interactions that I used to dread most. It was like an accidental experiment I did on myself that was a real eye opener. Maybe you can relate! Sometimes, it seems, the interactions that we take for granted are actually ones that keep us feeling our best.

A variety of social interactions makes us even happier. Diverse social interaction isn't merely about filling up our calendars; it turns out to be another substantial lever for boosting our happiness.

In the same PNAS study cited earlier, researchers also discovered that those who had a mix of different types of social interactions (with friends, family, coworkers, strangers) reported even higher levels of happiness, beyond just the quantity of socializing. This link between a diverse social life and well-being was consistent even after considering other factors like age, gender, income, and employment status.

In another study using data from the American Time Use survey, which looked at the daily activities of 19,197 Americans, researchers wanted to see if the variety of social interactions people had influenced their happiness. The findings showed, once again, that people who had a wider range of social interactions were generally happier.

Plus, mixing up your social circle seems to do wonders for your physical health too. People with more diverse social connections had fewer overnight stays in the hospital over the past year, even after considering other factors!

On top of making you feel good, small talk also improves active listening skills. It forces you to pay closer attention during chats that might not seem super exciting at first glance. This kind of practice helps you get better at catching those little details and the nonverbal communication people throw out there – stuff that's easy to miss if you don't practice.

It turns you into a more tuned-in listener, someone who can really get what others are trying to say, even when they're not laying it all out directly. One way to look at small talk is like doing some warm-up stretches before running a race. Engaging in small talk is a way to practice your conversational skills, setting you up to be even more on point when deeper, more important convos come your way.

Speaking of setting yourself up for success, small talk also is an important component to lay the foundation for deeper conversations and trust building. To be frank, you cannot have deep conversations and connections without small talk. It accounts for nearly one-third of our speech and is often referred to as a "social lubricator," which is interesting considering that people use the term "breaking the ice" when initiating conversations. It seems that without small talk, humans tend to have a barrier that needs to be overcome in order to establish a sense of trust.

One mental note that I try to remember when going into situations where small talk may be involved is to put out my hand, not my business card. So often, when I first started attending events, I would hand out business cards like candy, and would jump straight into what I offer.

I went into networking with the idea that if I didn't like small talk, nobody else did. We were all there for business, so I would just get straight down to it! For me, a successful event was one where I left with a purse filled with others' business cards.

Nowadays, I leave my business cards at home. It became a safety tool for me and even though I might have felt more comfortable leading with what I do, I wasn't building relationships; I was just collecting shallow connections.

Realizing this changed everything for me. I began to see small talk not as a tedious prelude to "real" conversations but as something more meaningful. By focusing on the person in front of me, rather than on what I wanted out of the interaction, I started to forge more meaningful, lasting relationships in my career. This shift from transactional networking to genuine connection has changed both my career and life and, honestly, made small talk a hell of a lot less stressful. Instead of just rehearsing the same elevator talk over and over, I started to see small talk as an opportunity to just simply say hello, it's nice to meet you. And truth be told, some of the most meaningful connections have started with the simplest of exchanges.

This points us to one more benefit of small talk: you may end up learning something new. From a knowledge perspective, polite chitchat could lead to new cultural insights, an introduction to an interesting new idea or tool (I've discovered so many fab books and podcasts this way), a discovery of local gems, or finding out about career opportunities you didn't know existed!

From a self-development perspective, small talk can teach you about people. While social anxiety loves to try and convince you that your true safety is in isolation and that people will judge you, the more you interact with other humans, the more you realize that most are kind, and are more likely to be wondering if they have something stuck in their teeth than to be silently critiquing you. Knowing that the vast majority of people have some degree of social anxiety can be an empowering way to go into your next interaction knowing that we really aren't all that different after all.

Small talk can also serve as a mirror, reflecting back to us aspects of who we are that we may not have been aware of, both positive and negative. Some build our self-confidence; others invite us to work on becoming better versions of ourselves.

This practice of stepping into small talk willingly can help to loosen the tight grip of social anxiety over time, showing us that socializing isn't as nightmarish as we had feared. As you can hopefully see by now, small talk has a unique way of broadening our horizons and changing how we think in unexpected ways. Every seemingly small interaction has the potential to teach us something new about the world, about others, and even about ourselves.

Strategies for Mastering Small Talk

Before we get into the nitty-gritty of how to become a chitchat champ, I want to start off by telling you to cut it out. Stop believing the lie that just because small talk feels hard or uncomfortable, that you're bad at it.

When I finally emerged without a mask after the pandemic and went to greet my producer, I threw my hands up awkwardly and admitted, "I don't know what I'm supposed to do here – do we shake hands or hug or fist bump each other?!" I felt awkward and rusty.

Like anything in life, small talk takes practice. You need to get yourself into the right headspace (preparation), learn how to keep your body relaxed and mind present, and how to exit more gracefully than "Uhm, I need to pee, bye!" (inevitably followed by a mental forehead slap).

Get into the Right Mindset

Just like athletes have a ritual before a big game, like jamming out to a certain playlist, doing specific stretches, or eating a certain meal, it can be super beneficial to figure out what you need to get into game mode for small talk. Some social interactions may happen spontaneously, but let's consider this scenario:

> *Lisa battles her alarm clock for the third snooze before the harsh reality of the time hits her. "Crap!" she exclaims, flinging the duvet aside and leaping out of bed in a frenzy. A frantic search through her wardrobe ends with a sniff-test-approved pair of work pants and a hastily gathered bun. Makeup is a lost cause today; she opts for a quick toothbrushing session instead. Disaster strikes— a blob of toothpaste lands on her blouse. "NO!" she cries out, dabbing at the stain before slipping into the nearest pair of shoes and dashing out the door.*
>
> *"Move it!" she pleads, stuck behind an endless stream of cars on the congested highway. A glance at the clock sends her pulse skyrocketing – her meeting is in five minutes, and she's still a nerve-wracking four minutes away. Horn blaring, heart thumping, she wills the traffic to part. Miraculously, it does, and she accelerates toward her goal. She slides into her parking spot with seconds to spare and rushes into the meeting, her heart a drumbeat in her chest, her body slick with sweat, craving the salvation of a strong coffee.*

I've been here, and maybe you have too. It's not a fun way to start your morning, and certainly not easy to dive into social interactions when your fight-or-flight mode is fully activated, especially if you already struggle with social anxiety.

The biggest problem with a scenario like this is that we may associate the stress that we feel in that moment with the people around us. For example, maybe Lisa's coworker Dave asked her how her drive in was, a benign question in other scenarios but one that makes Lisa want to snap at him, not because Dave did anything wrong, but because she's already overwhelmed and on edge. It's all too easy in these moments to let our stress spill over into our interactions, turning what could be a simple, pleasant exchange into something more tense and fraught.

Long term, these tense moments will inevitably turn into the lie we tell ourselves that we just don't like people, when truthfully we don't like feeling anxiety and stress around other people.

When I started performing on stage as a professional speaker in 2018, I quickly realized what I needed to feel my best. Because I'm an introvert, my social battery diminishes in approximately two hours (gosh, I wish I could upgrade it like my iPhone!). Therefore, if I do an hour keynote, I can handle one hour post-session to answer questions and socialize before I need to take a nap in my hotel room.

So I knew that I wouldn't be able to socialize with attendees prior to my talk. I needed that time to get ready in my hotel room, meditate, listen to some upbeat music, and just chill. I also try to arrive at the location with lots of time to spare so that I'm not feeling rushed or worried about being late. That way I can just breathe and focus on the task ahead of me.

Think about what it might be that you need before you socialize. Maybe you need to toss on some upbeat tunes or get your brain cranking with an interesting podcast. Maybe you're like me and need to have a moment to sit with a cup of coffee before engaging with others, or need to get to the parking lot of your office or hop on a Zoom call early to take a few breaths before that first hello.

If you know that you're going somewhere where small talk is likely, create your "game day" ritual that feels good and works for you to get yourself in the right mindset to interact.

Here are some ideas to build your No Fear Networking Warm-up:

- **Visualization:** Envision yourself as a confident, flawless networker. Imagine yourself confidently initiating conversations, listening actively, and responding with ease.

- **Create your "No Fear Networking" playlist:** Music has such a powerful impact on your emotions. My playlist starts with mellower, more calming tunes, followed by more upbeat, motivating jams to get me fired up right before I head out.

- **Practice mindfulness:** Spend 10–15 minutes in meditation to calm your mind and ground yourself. I personally love an app called Insight Timer because you can search for guided meditations specifically for managing social anxiety.

- **Physical warm-up:** Get your body moving with some light stretching, a short walk, or yoga poses to get rid of physical tension and increase endorphins. It's also good practice to learn how to manage the adrenaline rush that often comes with social interactions.

- **Power poses:** Try striking a power pose for a couple of minutes – like the superhero pose where you stand with your feet spread, hands on your hips, shoulders pulled back, and chin up, or the victory pose, where you throw your arms up in a V-shape, either standing or sitting. These poses could really pump up your confidence levels. Social psychologist Amy Cuddy in her TED Talk "Your Body Language May Shape Who You Are," highlights how these power poses can elevate your sense of empowerment, impacting your mental and physical state almost instantly.[5] What's more, the research shows that feeling powerful, whether it's real or just perceived, significantly changes our approach to networking.[6] Seeing yourself as a resource, not a burden, can revolutionize your networking game. It shifts your approach from taking to giving, enriching the quality of your interactions. So, by embracing power poses, you're not just boosting your confidence; you're also reshaping how you view yourself – as a valuable contributor. This mindset can transform your networking interactions, creating a virtuous cycle of positive exchanges.

- **Positive affirmations:** In the same vein, although it may feel a bit silly sometimes, pumping yourself up with positive affirmations can be a real game-changer for your confidence. Try crafting some personal pep-talk lines that speak to you and feel natural, like "I've got this and I'm fully prepped" or "I've done hard things and can do them again." Say them out loud to yourself in the mirror before you dive into a social setting or whenever you're feeling a bit shaky.

- **Arrive early:** Getting to your event early isn't just about being on time; it's about giving yourself time to mentally process your environment. By allowing some extra time, you can get comfortable with the space, people-watch a bit, and maybe even catch your breath in a washroom stall before everything kicks off. It's all about walking in feeling prepared and not rushed, which can make a huge difference in how you handle the event and engage with others. Plus, you'll get dibs on the best snacks or apps!

Here's what a typical "Mick's No Fear Networking Warm-up" would look like:

Step 1: Slow Start (Duration: As needed)

Begin the day with a warm coffee and a long, warm shower to wash away any jitters. While I'm at it, I play some calm tunes and slip into my comfy, fluffy robe to tackle hair and makeup. It's all about setting a slow, cozy pace to build on.

Step 2: Guided Meditation (10 minutes)

Next up, I dive into a 10-minute guided meditation focused on conquering social anxiety. I personally need guidance during meditations to help stop my brain from wandering too much. This helps me center my thoughts and calm my nerves. I wrap it up with a mist of Saje stress release spray to keep the zen vibes going. I've always found lavender and chamomile in particular to be super calming so I bring my little spray with me everywhere that I might need it, even in my purse to events!

Step 3: Energy Shift (Duration varies)

As I switch into my event outfit, I crank up more upbeat songs. The shift in music gets me into the right headspace for mingling, and at this point it's pretty much like a pregame before I enter the social "arena."

Step 4: Dance It Out (10 minutes)

Nothing pumps me up like a quick 10-minute dance party. I let loose, shake off any lingering stress, and boost my endorphins. Is it cute? Not really – my dancing is more like Elaine from *Seinfeld*, but it doesn't matter! What's important is that I feel the tension melting and every twerk attempt brings me a bit closer to feeling unstoppable. Just don't ask me for a tutorial on this one!

Step 5: Power Pose Pump (3 minutes)

With my spirits high, I spend 3 minutes striking some powerful poses to tap into my inner Beyoncé on stage singing to thousands of fans.

Step 6: Affirmation Boost (2 minutes)

I then anchor this energy with 2 minutes of strong, personal affirmations. Phrases like "I can do this" and "I am always safe and can exit whenever I need to" keep me charged and focused while still feeling secure.

Step 7: Smooth Send-Off (As needed)

Finally, I make sure to leave early enough to get to the venue with plenty of time to spare, ensuring I arrive as calm, cool, and collected as I can be.

Maybe your routine looks totally different than this, and that's okay! Not everybody finds value in meditation and essential oils, or maybe you would rather take a cold plunge instead of a warm shower to get pumped up. There is no right or wrong way to prepare for social gatherings, but knowing what you need to feel your best and crafting a routine that feels good is key.

It's all about personalizing your approach so that when you step into that room, you feel relaxed, confident, and ready to engage. So experiment a bit, tweak your routine as needed, and discover what truly helps you step into your social engagements with a little extra pep in your step.

Build Your Collection of Conversation Starters That Won't Make You Cringe

We're all guilty of panicking when we meet somebody new, especially at a professional event and blurting out the dreaded "So…what do you do?"

It can be so hard, especially when social anxiety kicks in, to think of anything else to say. There seems to be nothing more torturous in this world in that instant than an awkward silent moment. I would blurt out *anything* when that happens just to cut the silence.

But it's an awful question, isn't it? First, it's so general; it's very much like "Tell me about yourself!" The other person either doesn't know where to begin, or they give you a super-rehearsed version of their career story.

So how do you get around that? You build an arsenal of questions that feel authentic and genuine, but also allow you to get deeper in conversation, a place where those with social anxiety are known to thrive!

Let's start with the question "What do you do?" It probably feels most comfortable to you. Following are some fun work-related questions and conversation starters that you can ask instead that go a bit deeper and are easier and more enjoyable to answer.

Work-Related Questions

- How did you decide to become a [job title]?
- What are you working on right now that you're excited about?
- What are you most looking forward to in the next year?
- What's the best part of your job?
- Any big career goals that you're aiming for?

The key here with people you just met is to keep the vibes positive and also make sure to ask questions that don't come across as performative; they should flow naturally and be appropriate for the setting. Nobody wants to be caught off guard with a "what's your favorite pizza topping" question from someone they just met (although pepperoni and banana peppers if you're wondering).

Personal/Passion-Related Questions

- What are you passionate about outside of work?
- Have you come across any interesting books or podcasts lately? I'm always on the hunt for more!
- What's something that you're hoping to learn more about this year?
- What's one book you think everyone should read?

Asking more personal and passion-related questions can really transform a conversation, especially in rooms where most folks stick to the safe harbor of work talk.

Assuming everyone's main passion is their nine-to-five might not hit the mark for everyone. In fact, some people might be networking because they aren't happy with their current role and are looking for new opportunities! By steering the conversation toward personal interests, you're opening up a world where people can talk about what truly lights them up inside. This not only makes the chat more engaging but also allows connections to form on a more genuine level, far beyond just job titles and work achievements. It's a refreshing change that brings out more vibrant, memorable interactions because, let's face it, people love talking about what they love! This approach can really make you stand out in a sea of vanilla networkers.

Observational Questions

- What a gorgeous venue. Have you been here before?
- Is this your first time at [event name]?
- Is this your first time in [event city name]?
- Who are you most excited to hear speak, or which session can I not miss (if at an educational event or conference)?
- Have you tried any of the food/drinks here? Anything you'd recommend?
- You guys look like you're having the most fun here. Mind if I join you?
- I couldn't help but overhear your conversation about [topic]. Mind if I share some thoughts?

Observational questions are awesome because they use what's already happening around us to kickstart convos. They tap into a shared experience (the venue, location, crappy Wi-Fi, etc.), they can often feel like the most natural questions to ask or comments to make, and you may get an insider scoop on a speaker or location information that you might not have gotten otherwise! For the socially anxious professional, observational questions are a great bridge for deeper conversations.

Be Honest

- I'm trying to get better at networking, even though it's so outside my comfort zone. Have you learned any tricks that help calm nerves in places like this?
- I always feel a bit out of my element at these things. What helps you to chill out at events like this?
- I'm working on my networking skills tonight. On a scale of "awkward turtle" to "social butterfly," how am I doing so far?

- In case we both need a quick escape, what's your go-to excuse to leave a conversation at events like this?
- Hey, I'm [your name]. I have social anxiety but I'm here anyway doing this anyway! Mind if I join you?

When I feel super out of my element at an event, I've found that the best remedy for my social anxiety actually isn't to "fake it till I make it," but rather to be genuine and honest about how I'm feeling. They say that your vibe attracts your tribe, and I think being up front about your social anxiety can immediately cut through the traditional small talk and draw people closer to you.

Rather than making you appear weak, sharing that you have social anxiety can actually create an atmosphere where others can feel comfortable to drop their own networking mask and just talk human to human. It opens the door for others to share their own feelings and struggles. Plus, using a little self-deprecating humor keeps the conversation lighthearted, but still authentic.

I've found myself gravitating more toward questions and comments about my social anxiety over the past few years because it gives fears less power when they're spoken out loud, especially when you realize how many people you speak to are also battling their own social anxiety!

One question that somebody asked me at a speaker's party at a conference years ago still sticks out in my mind as one of the best networking questions to ask. I was chatting with a few speaker friends when one of them introduced me to John Hall, co-founder at Calendar.com, keynote speaker, author of a brilliant book called *Top of Mind,* and most importantly, just a really nice dude. Small talk usually feels forced and awkward, but I was in awe of how easily he made the conversation flow; it felt like I had known him forever. But what really impressed me was how, after we had been chatting for a bit, he stopped me and asked, "How can I be helpful to you?"

As a performer, I was used to having answers prepared for virtually any question, but that one really caught me off guard. "Wow," I replied, "I'll have to think about that one. Can I get back to you on that?" We parted ways, but that question lingered in my mind.

There are a few reasons why that question worked so well in a networking scenario. First off, it flips the whole script on the usual small talk. Instead of just skating on the surface with the usual "What do you do?" it dives right into something deeper. It turns a basic convo into an opportunity for real connection. Instead of just swapping business cards, you're actually talking about how you can make a difference for each other. That's pretty refreshing in the often transactional, salesy vibe of networking events.

Then there's the way this question puts the spotlight on the other person in a really empowering way. It's like saying, "Tell me what you need, and I'll see how I can help." That's not just nice; it's a game-changer. It gives the person a chance to think about what they actually need, like I did on my plane ride home, before following up with John on LinkedIn.

And let's talk about the trust factor. Offering help with no strings attached is incredibly rare in a world where people are constantly asking you for things. It's all about genuine support, not just what you can get out of the interaction, which honestly makes you stand out as someone people want to know, remember, and talk positively about, like I am right now.

I recently spoke with John, who emphasized the importance of setting reasonable boundaries. Having asked this "helpful" question countless times, he's learned that some people approach relationships transactionally, taking advantage of others' help. To navigate this, John still asks the question but is mindful of what he commits to, ensuring his interactions lead to genuine relationships. This approach allows him to assist people thoughtfully and focus on those who align with his values.

He believes that when both parties genuinely want each other to succeed, the best outcomes naturally follow. This principle has positively influenced his career, marriage, and friendships, all of which have thrived with this approach in mind.[7]

Questions ≠ Conversation

Questions are great, but remember that you're having a conversation, not conducting an interview. There have been a few times when I've been chatting with somebody and after the first couple of questions, it started to feel intrusive, or like they were running through an exercise rather than genuinely seeking answers. And when I sense inauthenticity, my brain yells, "Abort conversation!" Maybe you've been there, too.

So how do you make sure you're engaging rather than interrogating? Here are some tips to keep your questions from becoming a rapid-fire Q&A.

Take turns sharing and be a little vulnerable: Sometimes, sharing an opinion or personal story related to the topic can make the exchange feel more like a two-way street. It shows you're not just focused on them answering your questions but are willing to contribute, too.

And if you're cringing right now worried about how much to share with a stranger, consider Carole Robin's "15% rule." For example, using one of the "be honest" questions above, "Hey, I'm [your name]. I have social anxiety but I'm here anyway doing this anyway! Mind if I join you?"

I'm disclosing that I have social anxiety to the person I'm speaking to. Does this make me feel a bit vulnerable to disclose this? Absolutely. Does it freak me out or could it repel the other person? Probably not. So this would be within my 15% outside of my comfort zone.

Now, let's imagine that the person I'm speaking to replies: "Fellow anxious networker here! I would love it if you'd join me, I was just rehearsing excuses to leave!"

So don't be afraid to step a little bit outside your usual comfort zone. It can make conversations feel more real and pave the way for deeper, more meaningful connections.

React to answers: Show you're really listening by responding thoughtfully. A quick "Wow, I hadn't thought of that!" or "That's a great point!" can make the conversation richer. This not only keeps the chat flowing but also lets them know you genuinely value their take on things, encouraging them to open up even more.

You can also use questions to dig deeper into their responses. If they mention an interesting detail, follow up with, "Can you tell me more about that?" or "What was that like?"

Focus on "What" Questions, Rather Than "Why" Questions

According to Dr. Carole Robin, asking "why" questions can often lead people to overthink and feel the need to justify or defend their actions. This type of question can unintentionally cause feelings of judgment and make individuals more likely to respond defensively.[0]

Instead, focus on what, when, where, or how questions, like:

"Which part of this project are you most excited about?"
"When did you first get into this field?"
"Where do you see [your industry] heading in the next few years?"

These types of questions help people open up and share more freely, turning your chat into an honest, enjoyable conversation rather than a tense interrogation.

Remember, a conversation should feel like a genuine exchange of ideas, where questions help guide the flow but don't dominate it. Keep it real and leave room for unexpected tangents. You might uncover something far more interesting than what you initially set out to ask!

Listening to Connect and the Art of Engagement

Admit it, sometimes when you're "listening," you're actually just waiting for your turn to talk. I know because I've been there too. In fact, I didn't really start to get better at it until I had to shut up and listen while interviewing people for this book!

In this section, we're going to master the subtle art of truly tuning in to what others are saying, without drifting off to your grocery list or trying to recall what the heck the person's name is. Prepare to flex those listening muscles (yes, they exist!) and transform every chat into a more meaning-ful dialogue.

But let's address the elephant in the room. When you're anxious, it's tough to focus on the person speaking. Your mind might be racing with thoughts like "Do I look nervous?" or "What do I say next to avoid an awk-ward silence?" The thought traffic in your head isn't just distracting; it drowns out the other person's words, making active listening almost impossible.

But here's a bit of good news: getting better at this stuff is totally doable. Remember that networking is a muscle, and so is active listening. You can and will get better at focusing over time if you allow yourself to practice more.

And the best part is that the more that you learn to focus your attention on the person you're speaking with, the less time you'll have to listen to your anxious thoughts. So let's get into it!

According to Julian Treasure, an expert on sound and communication and TED Talk speaker with millions of views worldwide, there are four steps involved in active listening, a process that he calls the RASA framework,[9] which stands for:

Receive: This is where you put all your focus on the person talking. No sneaky glances at your phone or drifting off daydreaming. Lock in, listen to their words, and watch their body language too. It's about catching every little detail, not just the words.

Appreciate: While you're paying attention, throw in some nods or a thoughtful "mm-hmm" or "right." These little signals fire back to the speaker that you're not just standing there waiting for them to finish talking, but you're truly engaged. It makes them feel heard and valued, and keeps the conversation flowing.

Summarize: Echo their points back in your own words. It shows you're not just hearing them, but really understanding what they're saying. Plus, it clears up any potential miscommunication right off the bat. Let's look at this one in an example, where you're talking with a friend who just led their first major project at work.

Friend "Leading that project was intense! Everything was running smoothly at first, but then we hit a snag with our software just before the deadline. It was a rough first project, but we pulled it off and solved it just in time."

You "Whoa, that sounds crazy! That's a roller coaster to have a last minute hiccup like that, so glad that you were still able to pull it off!"

Ask: Ask follow-up questions to show that you've really listened. This step helps you stay engaged and shows genuine interest in what they're saying. It keeps the conversation flowing and ensures you're getting the full picture. Plus, asking thoughtful questions shows them you value their input and gives them a chance to share even more. Use some of the question tips in the previous section to figure out what to ask to encourage your conversation partner to continue.

With the RASA framework nailed down, it's time to up your game with some engagement techniques that will keep the convo flowing. Active listening helps you tune in, but engagement is where the magic happens, turning the chat into something that you walk away with the warm fuzzies instead of cringing.

One of the biggest challenges for people with social anxiety in social situations is relying on safety behaviors that can come across as disinterest – like crossing your arms, avoiding eye contact, or standing too far away from the group. These actions might help us feel secure, but they often send the wrong message to the people we're trying to connect with. The key is recognizing these habits and working toward body language that invites more genuine connections and makes others feel welcome.

So I created a simple, easy-to-remember acronym that I jot down on my palm before events to help me make a positive impression on the people I talk to: IMPACT, which stands for:

Interest (eye contact): For me, this is by far the hardest one, yet it seems to be a key component of conversations (unless you're a contestant on *Love Is Blind*). So how do you get better at this? According to Arlin Cuncic, author of *The Anxiety Workbook*, there are a few strategies that you can try. If direct gaze is too stressful, you can look near the eyes, like their nose, forehead, or eyebrows; use the 50/70 technique, where you maintain eye contact for 50% of the time while speaking, 70% while listening; or use the triangle technique, where instead of looking away or down after making eye contact, you look at another spot of the face (imagine a triangle with their eyes and nose, for example).[10]

Mirroring: Mirroring is when you repeat or imitate someone's words or behavior. It's often used to build trust and make the other person feel understood, encouraging them to share more. In his bestselling book, *Never Split the Difference*, former FBI hostage negotiator Christopher Voss, writes, "By repeating back what people say, you trigger this mirroring instinct and your counterpart will inevitably elaborate on what was just said and sustain the process of connecting."[11] Here's an example of what mirroring might look like in conversation:

Person A	"I've been working a lot on improving engagement on LinkedIn."
You	"Improving engagement on LinkedIn? I'd love to hear about your approach! What strategies have you tried so far?"

Posture (open posture): You want to make sure that your posture is saying, "I'm approachable and receptive," not "Back off, or I'll bite you!" Make sure that your body is turned fully toward the person you're speaking to, not turned away like you're about to escape. Avoid crossing your arms, because this can send the message that you're in defense mode. Keep your arms and hands relaxed and by your side or holding onto your drink or food.

Leaning forward can also signal to the person that you're interested in what they're saying and want to hear more. But remember that this is a conversation, not a performance, so while these things are good to know, try not to robotically position yourself and spend time pondering whether your posture is open enough. Just try to relax your body and be present in the moment.

Avoid interrupting: This is something that I struggle with, and can be so hard for some people. When you get excited about a topic, you disagree with the person speaking, or your social anxiety is pushing you to keep the conversation moving and avoid silences, it can be difficult to truly listen and wait to speak. But even if you're buzzing with excitement or have a strong opinion, try and take a breath and actively listen. This simple act shows that you genuinely value their perspective and creates a respectful space for conversation to unfold.

Cues (nodding): Don't overdo it and look like a bobblehead, but nod every now and then to show that you're following along and understand what's being said. It gives the speaker a nudge to keep going and shows them you're listening and interested in the conversation.

Tone (facial expressions and voice tone): Maintain a warm, friendly expression to keep the vibes positive. If you're prone to RBF (resting bitch face) like I am, be aware of that and make sure that you're not scowling while you're chatting. Match your tone and intonation to the conversation's mood. If it's serious, use a calm tone, and if it's upbeat, bring a little energy with a rising intonation.

Next time you're chatting with someone, try to apply one or two of these techniques. Whether it's holding eye contact or giving a few nods, these small steps will help you walk away feeling like this whole networking thing isn't so bad after all. Stay present and curious, and most importantly, be yourself!

How to End a Conversation

Besides starting a conversation, the hardest part for me about networking is figuring out when and how to end it. I've had those awkward moments where I'm not sure if I'm staying too long or ducking out too early, leaving me fumbling internally, trying to figure out how to say goodbye. So today we're going to nail down the art of wrapping things up smoothly, whether you're chatting with a new connection at a networking event or catching up with an old friend.

Learn to spot the signals that it's time to wind down and end the conversation on a high note so you both walk away feeling good about it. Let's dive into the not-so-easy art of saying "So nice to meet you, gotta run!"

Signs It's Time to Say Goodbye

The trickiest part about signs that it's time to end a conversation is that so many people worry that ending a conversation might be viewed as rude that they often try *not* to give out signals that it's time to cut things short.

However, here are some subtle and not-so-subtle signs that it's time to end the conversation and make your exit:

- **There's a natural pause:** A lull in the conversation can signal that it's time to say goodbye.
- **Lack of eye contact:** The other person might start looking around the room, at their watch or phone, or just seem a bit distracted as they figure out their exit strategy.
- **Body language:** They might start moving away from you and toward the door, shifting their weight, or fidgeting more.
- **Verbal cues:** The person might seem to repeat thoughts or summarize the conversation, or say things like "Well, it was great meeting you…" or "Okay, well I need to get to…"
- **There's a hard stop:** Sometimes people either voice a time constraint or, if you have a 15 minute Zoom meeting scheduled with the person, assume that they would like to end the conversation by the allotted time.

But beyond knowing the signs that it's time to end a conversation, how do you get more comfortable with the idea of exiting? One of the best pieces of advice that I've heard about this comes from Rich Mulholland, founder of Missing Link and a global public speaker who manages to crush it while battling social anxiety. According to Rich, the hardest part of networking is knowing the "dance," when to interrupt and when to exit and move onto the next person.[12] In his words:

> "It was only at an event where I sat back and watched people that I realized that there was a dance. It was a lot like the Scottish 'stripping the willows' dance where people went from partner to partner. In any group there were their roles, 'the leaver,' the 'hang-abouters,' and the joiners. I observed that if two people were chatting and someone new joined them, one person then had 'permission' to depart. That leaver became the new joiner for another group. As I processed this for a few minutes I observed another person join the conversation. They all spoke for a while, but then the previous 'hang-about(s)' could leave and the previous joiner became the 'hang-about.' It was like a dance everyone knew that I didn't. And then the penny dropped for me."

Seeing networking as a dance with moves, rather than locking onto a conversation with the one person you know and hanging on to them all night for dear life (guilty!), or feeling guilty for "abandoning" a conversation, was a huge revelation for Rich and made offstage banter much easier. As Rich puts it, "By joining I allowed the other person to leave without being rude. It's interruption-as-a-service. Understanding this removed a lot of my social anxiety as I realized that I was just a part of a bigger dance."

For me, that mindset shift, away from abandonment to interruption and exiting as a service, has been a game changer. It allows people to navigate conversations with confidence and ease, making networking events feel more natural. Rich's approach reframed my understanding of social interactions, helping me see networking as a more fun dance rather than a stressful obligation.

Now let's talk about what to say when you "dance away" from a conversation. Dr. Charlynn Ruan, clinical psychologist and CEO of Thrive Psychology Group, shares a few ideas for exiting phrases in an article[13]:

"I need to head out in a bit, but let's catch up soon."

> **Why it works:** This phrase shows a willingness to maintain the connection while clearly signaling that you're wrapping up.

"I'd love to chat more, but I have to run to my next thing."

> **Why it works:** Here, you're emphasizing your interest in the conversation while conveying that other commitments are calling. It highlights your busy schedule without undermining the value of the current chat.

"This has been a real eye-opener. Let's do it again soon."

> **Why it works:** Expressing genuine appreciation for the insights that they've shared encourages leaves the other person feeling valued.

"Always a joy chatting with you, but I've got to dash"

> **Why it works:** I love this one. It recognizes the positive vibes of the interaction while sharing that it's time to move on. It's friendly and lighthearted, making the exit feel natural.

"I've loved our chat, but I should let you get back to your day."

> **Why it works:** This wraps up the conversation by demonstrating empathy while gracefully closing the interaction.

These exit lines are your secret weapons for wrapping things up smoothly without that awkward guilt. They help you shift gears gracefully so you leave a positive impression while freeing up your time for other connections.

And remember Maya Angelou's words: "People will forget what you said, people will forget what you did, but people will never forget how you made them feel."[14] Treat the "dance" of networking and small talk as a chance to leave others with a positive first impression that social anxiety can make challenging.

7 | Harnessing the Power of Online Networking: LinkedIn and Beyond

While there are some real perks to meeting people face to face, like decoding all those helpful cues from tone and body language, the digital world offers some sweet advantages too – like rocking your comfiest attire while making connections from your favorite spot on the sofa.

For those navigating social anxiety, mixing in-person and online networking can be a game changer, giving you control over how and when you engage, making the whole process a little less daunting and a lot more doable.

Navigating LinkedIn

Networking doesn't always have to be face to face, although there are some clear advantages to meeting people in person, like reading somebody's body language, making an immediate impression, and having a new shared experience of whatever event you're at.

LinkedIn provides an opportunity to connect with people around the world, right from the comfort of your own home or desk. I often refer to it as "The World's Largest Networking Event" because any and every person you could want to meet likely has a profile on LinkedIn.

But maybe you haven't had the best experience on the platform, maybe your inbox is filled with spammy messages and recruiters trying to lure you to irrelevant jobs.

I get it. I was there too. I thought LinkedIn was just a place to stick your resume and call it a day. That was until the winter of 2016, when I was laid off from the startup I was working for. With bills piling up and nothing to lose, I started posting more on LinkedIn and spending more time reaching out to people in my community.

And something crazy happened. People…actually cared. They were becoming invested in my stories about navigating the job search with interviews gone wrong and overcoming the grief and shame of job loss.

Suddenly, my inbox was filling up with people sending me links, making introductions to people they knew were hiring, and then a company that had been following my posts reached out, interviewed me, and created a new position just for me.

Seemingly overnight, I went from broke jobseeker to career blogger with thousands of followers. But this isn't to brag about my "influencer" journey, because I'm literally a socially anxious, overcaffeinated gal from Ottawa. But I had discovered something important. True connection is possible in a digital world, and you don't need to be famous, rich, or well-connected to build a community.

So, are you ready to knock the dust off your profile and turn it from passive to magnetic? Let's dive into creating a LinkedIn profile that pulls in opportunities and builds genuine connections, making sure you're not just another face in the newsfeed but a beacon attracting the right kind of attention.

Crafting a Magnetic Profile

To create a space that truly feels like you on LinkedIn, imagine again that you're at a networking event. What are you wearing? What vibes are you giving off? How do you want people to perceive you? What do you want people to walk away knowing about you and your goals for the future.

Now, open LinkedIn and look at your profile. Does it match your energy and personality? Does it clearly demonstrate your experience and communicate your ambitions and values? Would a visitor leave your profile having an accurate impression of you?

Here's the thing. People are looking at your profile. Anytime you apply for a job, have a conversation with a potential client, or meet somebody at an in-person event, I can promise you that they are likely scoping you out on LinkedIn either before or after your interaction. So spend time updating your profile to reflect who you are and what you want more of, to make sure what they see is what you want them to.

Profile Prime Real Estate

The most important part of your LinkedIn profile is the part that people see before scrolling: your cover image, profile photo, and headline. I call this your profile prime real estate, because most people will only see this part of your LinkedIn profile before clicking to something else. You need to make it count!

Your Cover Image

Let's start with your cover image. This is an area that stumps most people, who usually leave it as the default image. That's kind of like the equivalent of the egg for your profile photo that used to show up on Twitter (now X). It can give off the impression that you either don't care enough to optimize the space, or you are an AI-generated profile created to spam or scam. Surely neither of those impressions are ones you want to make, so let's chat about some ideas for this space:

Show Off What You Do   Think of your LinkedIn cover image as your career collage. It should scream "you" in all the right ways. If you're in a creative field like graphic design, show off your talent with an image that showcases your favorite work.

If you're a real estate agent, try a photo of you handing over house keys to a new client. I recognize that some careers are trickier than others, but if most of your work is online, for example, include a "candid" photo of yourself running a meeting or speaking to your computer.

With a little creativity, photos can be found that work for nearly every job position.

Tell People What You Want More of   Use this space to drop hints about where you want to be or what you want to accomplish.

When I first started speaking, I used a photo of me on stage as my cover image to convey that I was a speaker and that I was interested in speaking gigs. It worked like an absolute charm.

It may sound a bit silly, but you need to make it crystal clear what you want to achieve. You're painting a picture not just with words, but with visuals that pack a punch. If you're gunning for leadership roles, why not use a shot where you're leading a team meeting or presenting at a big conference?

Remember, subtlety is not your friend here; be as obvious as a flashing billboard. It's about putting your ambitions out there in the universe and making sure everyone knows what you're aiming for.

Celebrate Your Wins or Announce Upcoming Projects   Got something to celebrate? It's time to get over the idea that humility means never sharing what you've achieved or what you're excited about. Put it front and center. This could be a snapshot from a keynote you delivered, an award ceremony where you were recognized, or a banner from a major publication that you've contributed to. Currently, my focus is on this book, so I've included a photo of the book cover in that space. Share whatever is important to you at the moment.

And speaking of "in the moment," remember that your goals, wins, and position may change, so be sure to update your cover image accordingly and keep it fresh. You also want to make sure that the photo that you include is high quality (no low-res logos from a quick Google search!), and that it also works well on mobile devices. Also remember to look at the placement of the profile image and make sure that it coordinates well with your cover photo. The last thing you want is for your profile picture to awkwardly block an important part of your cover image, like the title of your book or the award in your hand.

Your Profile Photo

First impressions count, and on LinkedIn it all starts with your profile photo. Let's make sure yours isn't just good, but great! Here's how to snap that perfect picture that says, "I'm a professional" and "I'm friendly" all at once.

Frame it like Goldilocks (just right): Make sure your face takes up about 40–60% of the frame. Just like at a networking event, you want to be clearly visible, not too close, not too far. This setup shows your full face without feeling too crowded or awkward.

Get your (approachable) pose on: Use open body language. Think about how you'd show up at a networking event: body facing forward, smiling, arms relaxed.

Quality counts: Always use high-quality photos. Blurry or pixelated images just don't cut it, but if you're using a smartphone, don't let that stop you! I promise you have all you need to take a great photo. Get a coworker or family member to snap a shot of you, or order a cheap tripod and remote on Amazon to take your own photos.

Be the (solo) star: This is your professional spotlight, so keep it solo. Group photos can be confusing to people trying to place you by face.

Light it right: Good lighting makes a huge difference. Natural light works best, giving your skin a soft, even look. If you're taking your own photos, remember to be facing the sun, because having the sun behind you will create weird shadows and darkness that makes it hard to see your face.

Just like with your cover image, remember to update your photo every couple of years, or whenever your appearance changes significantly (like you grew a mustache or dyed your hair purple). Keeping your photo current is important so that when people meet you in person, they'll recognize you instantly. Having an inconsistent look offline can affect the trust factor.

Headline Hack

Creating a magnetic headline that captures who you are in one concise phrase is no easy task. That's why I've created an easy to use method called the PPP Identity Formula that will help you to capture the essence of you for both your LinkedIn headline and for in-person networking events:

PPP Identity Formula = Position + Passion + Purpose

Here's what it might look like in practice:

1. Start with your position; your current role, or, if you work for yourself, what you're best known for, such as Expert Copywriter.

2. Next, add your passion. This could be your industry, it might connect to your current role, or it could be a more general passion that helps to humanize you – Creative Ad Campaigns, for instance.

3. Last, share your purpose, or the impact of your services. The key here (and I can't emphasize this enough) is to make it as simple as humanly possible – for example, Helping Brands Tell Better Stories.

Now putting it all together, your headline might look like this:

> Expert Copywriter | Creative Ad Campaigns | Helping Brands Tell Better Stories

My favorite thing about this headline is that it includes something from the realms of psychology and copywriting called the magic of threes. This is a principle that suggests that when information is delivered in groups of threes, it becomes more memorable, is easier for the human brain to process, and leaves a more lasting impression.

This is a good principle to keep in mind as you meet people in person as well and they say, "So, tell me about yourself."

Building Your LinkedIn About Section: Who, Why, What, and How

After your profile photo, cover image, and headline, your About section is often the first thing people see when they visit your profile. It's your chance to create a personal connection right from the start. Again, if we reimagine LinkedIn as the world's largest networking event, think of your "about" description as your digital handshake, an opportunity to share your passions, values, and experiences that define who you are and where you're going.

Let's break down my formula for writing a powerful LinkedIn About section.

Who You Are

Start with a brief introduction that highlights what sets you apart in your industry. This is your chance to make a strong first impression, so be clear and concise. Be sure to begin with a captivating sentence that grabs attention and encourages readers to click the "see more" option. This could be a bold statement, a thought-provoking question, or a powerful quote – for example, "Ever wondered how a single LinkedIn profile can transform your career? I help professionals unlock that potential every day."

In this first part of your "about" description, mention your current job title and the company you work for. If you're self-employed or a freelancer, describe your business or the services you provide, such as "I am a LinkedIn Trainer and Coach with over 10 years of experience in helping professionals optimize their LinkedIn presence."

Why You Do What You Do

Before delving into what you do in more detail, connect on a deeper level with your reader by sharing your why: your passion, your core values, and the story behind your career journey. Explain how your experiences have shaped who you are and why you are passionate about your work. Discuss what drives you and what you believe in professionally: "I believe in the power of community and the transformative impact of a magnetic personal brand. My mission is to help professionals unlock their full potential by leveraging the full potential of LinkedIn."

Connect the dots of your career journey. Share key moments, decisions, or turning points that led you to where you are today. This helps your reader to understand the "why" behind your career choices and become more emotionally invested in your story and success.

Here's my own example: "After being laid off from a tech start up right before my 30th birthday, I posted on LinkedIn. I had nothing to lose. Then something incredible happened. People became invested in my story and journey from jobseeker to running my own business. My inbox exploded with opportunities that I never thought possible for somebody like me. I felt called to share the lessons, formulas, and strategies that worked for me to help others take control of their career destiny."

Describe your impact on others. Explain how your work makes a difference for your clients, colleagues, or industry: "My clients often see significant improvements in their online visibility, growth in their network, and an increase in opportunities that they are seeking. Knowing that I can contribute to someone's growth in any way is what keeps me fired up about my work."

What You Have to Offer

Very simply, this is a clear description of your services or products. Don't use big, fancy words or overcomplicate this.

Again, imagine that you're at a networking event and somebody has asked you what kind of services you offer. Keep it concise and direct, so that even if the reader isn't your ideal client or customer, they might be able to refer your LinkedIn profile to people who are. Bullet points and white space are your friend here, to make it more digestible, like this:

> I offer a range of services designed to help you maximize your LinkedIn presence and leverage social media for professional growth. My services include:
>
> - Personalized LinkedIn Coaching: One-on-one coaching sessions tailored to your specific needs and goals, helping you optimize your LinkedIn profile and strategy.
> - LinkedIn Profile Optimization: Comprehensive reviews and enhancements of your LinkedIn profile to ensure it stands out and attracts the right audience.
> - Corporate LinkedIn Training Workshops: Customized workshops for teams and organizations to improve their LinkedIn skills and strategies.
> - LinkedIn Strategy Consulting: Expert advice on creating and implementing effective LinkedIn strategies that align with your business objectives.
> - Speaking Engagements on LinkedIn: Engaging and informative talks on the latest trends and best practices in LinkedIn.
> - LinkedIn Content Creation and Strategy: Help in developing compelling content and strategies that boost your visibility and influence on LinkedIn.

How to Get in Touch

Provide your contact information and encourage readers to connect with you. Make it easy for them to reach out to you. Make sure to include your preferred contact methods, like this:

> "Feel free to connect with me here on LinkedIn or email me at [email address]."

Finally, clearly state what you want the reader to do next. This could be connecting, emailing, or visiting your website:

> "Whether you need personalized LinkedIn coaching, a speaker for your next event, or just want to discuss social media trends, I'm always excited to discuss new opportunities. My inbox is always open!"

So there you have it, the core pieces of your LinkedIn profile that you can optimize to elevate your networking online. Now let's dig into who you should connect with.

Connecting with the Right People

Before you start connecting willy-nilly on LinkedIn, pump the brakes and ask yourself, "What's my endgame here"? Understanding precisely what you're aiming for with your LinkedIn connections will not only save you a ton of time but also make sure you're connecting with people who can genuinely rocket your career or business to new heights.

Define Your Networking Goals for LinkedIn

Climbing the career ladder: Eyeing a swanky new job title? Look for recruiters, dream companies to work for, and those elusive insiders. Connect with them and you'll be the first to find out about new gigs and insider company scoops.

Growing your brand: If you're hustling to scale your biz, connect with potential clients, job candidates, and suppliers. Don't forget to tap into investors and partners who are on the lookout for exciting opportunities – just like yours.

Boosting your brainpower: Hungry for knowledge? Connect with thought leaders and industry experts. Start conversations, swap ideas, and maybe find a mentor!

Mastering the Art of the Connection Request

So you've defined your goals and created a list of people on LinkedIn that you want to connect with. Now what?

First things first: ditch the default "I'd like to connect with you on LinkedIn" message and don't just send a connection request without a message at all. If you click connect and it automatically shoots off the request without the message option, simply go back to the person's profile and add your message to the pending request.

Also, don't use AI or a spammy generator tool that adds a message that looks like this: "Hi there, I love the work that you're doing at [insert company name here] and want to connect to learn more."

If you think people don't know what you're up to...we know what you're up to. Don't sour a first impression by using automation tools that seem more convenient. Personalizing your connection request shows that you're genuinely interested in the person, not just boosting your contact count.

Here are some quick tips to make the most of your (very limited) space to add a message:

Make it specific: Did you listen to a podcast the person was on or see a conference they spoke at? Mention it! Mentioning a specific link can make your request feel more relevant – for instance, "I noticed we both graduated from UCLA and have a passion for copywriting."

Compliment their work: If something specific about their career or a project they've worked on caught your eye, let them know. This could be an article they wrote or a presentation they gave, such as "I was really impressed by your latest article on using AI to become a better writer. It sparked some new ideas for my own work!"

Explain what's in it for them: Make it clear why you're reaching out. Are you inspired by their work and want to keep up to date on their latest insights? Do you share similar professional interests or goals? Say it!

Keep it short and sweet: Your message should be straight to the point. Respect their time by keeping your request brief but meaningful. For example, you could say, "Hi, Jordan. I loved your presentation at yesterday's webinar on innovative marketing strategies. I'd love to share some thoughts on a potential collab! Cheers, Alex."

If you need more space to add context and simply can't fit it into the connection request space, consider sending an InMail message instead. You can do this by either signing up for a premium account so you can send a certain amount of InMail messages per month to people you aren't connected to, or by checking on the person's profile to see if it's an "open profile." An open profile means that you are able to send an InMail message without needing a premium account or using InMail credits.

Follow Up After Connection Request Acceptance

If they accept your request, a thoughtful follow-up can help to start building a relationship. Send a thank you message expressing gratitude for accepting the connection, and then propose a next step.

Something that I believe in strongly in networking is that the initiator needs to take the lead on structuring the conversation. So if you are the one requesting to connect, for example, suggest a low-pressure next step that could benefit both of you, like sharing an article you think they'd find interesting or proposing a quick Zoom chat. Using the previous example, a connection request follow-up could look something like this:

Hi Jordan,

Thanks for accepting my connection request! I appreciated your approach during the webinar and I'm fired up thinking about the possibilities of using some of your strategies in my own work. I would love to work with you one-on-one. Would you be open to a 15-minute Zoom call next week to chat more?

Looking forward to hopefully working together!

Cheers, Alex

There are a few reasons why I like getting and sending messages like this:

It feels personal: Not only did Alex personalize the connect request, but he also reiterated where he met Jordan in the follow-up. It makes it feel intentional and thoughtful.

Clear intent: There's no "let me pick your brain" vibes in the follow-up. General requests often fall flat because you are asking for something without even knowing the person yet, but also there is no clear intent. What does this "brain picking" entail? Fifteen minutes of my time? Two hours? Do I need to prepare or meet you somewhere?

If you are going to make any sort of ask, make sure that the expectations are absolutely clear. That's why "Would you be open to a 15-minute Zoom call next week?" works so well, because the length of time, location, and date are all laid out clearly for the other person.

Leveraging LinkedIn Networking Tools

LinkedIn Search and Filters

Screeeeech! Let's rewind for a minute before we dive deeper into how to foster relationships via LinkedIn Messenger, because before you connect, you need to know how to actually find the right people on LinkedIn.

First, let's start with the basics. At the top of your LinkedIn mobile or desktop app, you'll find a search bar. This is the gateway to begin your networking journey. Here, you can type in keywords, job titles, companies, or names of people who you want to connect with if you know them by name already.

From here, you can filter the "people" results by first, second, or third connections, mutual connections, followers of specific people, people who are actively hiring, locations, current and past companies, school, industry, profile language, and service categories. The options are extensive and constantly evolving.

Overwhelmed by the number of choices? Let's see how this might look in practice:

Kara is tired of working in retail and wants to transition to a role in the tech industry. She's excited for change but overwhelmed by the sheer number of people hanging out on LinkedIn. So she uses LinkedIn search tools to make networking online feel more manageable.

Kara begins her search by entering the keywords "Marketing Manager" into the search bar. Next, she refines her search by choosing her location to be close to home. She targets her dream companies to work for like Google and Microsoft. She chooses "Information Services and Technology" from the industry section.

Then she filters for alumni from her university because having the same educational background might be helpful for her to break the ice.

By filtering for and connecting with people who can help her land her dream job, Kara is using her time on LinkedIn more intentionally, and it helps her feel more comfortable to reach out with a purpose.

LinkedIn Messaging Tools

Alright, now that you've found your people, let's talk about making the first move without feeling like you're cold-calling. There are two types of messages that you can send on LinkedIn: InMail and direct.

InMail: If you don't have a direct connection, LinkedIn's InMail is how you'll send a message to the person you're trying to reach. It lets you message second and third connections, but remember that this is a premium feature, so you either need to have a premium account to send one or the person must have what's called an open profile. When crafting an InMail, keep it concise and focused. This is going to be especially true because the person hasn't accepted a connection request from you. Start with why you're reaching out and what you admire about their career or expertise. Be clear about what you're asking for, like this:

Subject: Let's Chat About Fear of Rejection?

Hi Adam,

I hope this finds you well! I'm Michaela, and I've been really diving deep into the root causes of social anxiety lately. I've been following your impressive work, especially your thoughts on fear of rejection – super insightful!

I'm reaching out because I feel there's a lot we could talk about and possibly collaborate on for my upcoming book. I'd love to chat more on a quick call and see if we might align. Would you be up for that? I can work around your schedule and keep it at 15 minutes.

Thanks a lot for considering this! Looking forward to hopefully chatting soon.

Love and coffee, Michaela

Direct messaging: Start with something personal, but not weirdo-vibes personal. Noticed they went to the same school or volunteered for an awesome cause? Maybe you loved an article they wrote or shared? Start there: "Hey Adam, I see we both have a passion for the psychology of social anxiety, and I really enjoyed your thoughts on fear of rejection. Would love to chat more about this! Do you have 15 minutes in the next few weeks for a quick Zoom call?"

From your LinkedIn inbox, you can also access tools like adding media (gifs, photos, docs, etc.), adding emojis to messages, sending voice messages (great for adding a more personal touch), or starting or schedule a video call.

But I can read your socially anxious mind right now, and I get it. It's nice to know what tools are available, but usually when it comes to social anxiety, the problem isn't technical, it's emotional and/or psychological. It's not that you don't know how to use LinkedIn; it's that the idea of reaching out to strangers, even online, is scary.

When you're feeling hesitant about reaching out, keep in mind that the worst response you can get is no response at all – and that's totally okay! When I think back at all the messages that I've sent and received on LinkedIn, you know which ones ended up mattering most? The authors who said yes to an interview, the agency that hired me for a huge campaign, the people I admired who went on to become mentors, sources of referrals, even friends.

There are so many potential opportunities waiting for you on the other side of fear, so let's chat about how to build up the courage to connect on LinkedIn.

Start small: If initiating a private conversation feels daunting, begin with liking or commenting on posts from people you want to connect with more regularly. This can naturally lead into more direct messages, since you're already having back-and-forth conversations.

Also try sending messages to connections who are already within your comfort zone, such as classmates or colleagues from current or past jobs. Just getting into the habit of sending messages and requesting connections can boost your confidence when reaching out to new people.

Set clear intentions: Whether it's seeking advice, discussing a shared interest, or exploring job opportunities, having a clear purpose before you reach out can be helpful for battling social anxiety because it gives structure to the conversation and makes sure you're both on the same page from the start. For me, the struggle socially is when there is no structure at all and the expectations are unclear, like when somebody sends me a message that says something like "Hi, how are you?"

Those kinds of messages can make the wheels in my brain spin into overdrive. Are we about to dive deep into existential questions; do you want to hear about how my toddler's potty training is going; or is it just polite small talk? That's why, when you're reaching out, being clear and specific can really take the edge off.

Do it regularly: Psychologists say that it takes about 21 days to form a habit, so imagine the progress you could make if you commit to reaching out on LinkedIn daily for just three weeks. Decide on a specific number of people you'll reach out to each day or week, block out a time in your calendar for sending out your connection requests on LinkedIn, and incorporate it into your daily or weekly routine. There is no right or wrong number to aim for; just make sure that it feels sustainable for you and your current schedule. You'll likely find after the first week or two that reaching out isn't actually so terrifying after all!

How to Rekindle Conversations on LinkedIn: The CHAT Formula

One situation that many people find awkward or uncomfortable on LinkedIn is reaching out to somebody via Messenger with whom you haven't spoken in a while, even years.

To combat the nerves when it comes to reconnecting, I've created the CHAT Formula, which is something that works well for LinkedIn, email, or any messaging tool online. Here's how to format your message using this formula:

C – Compliment: Start your message by reconnecting on a positive note. Highlight something you've seen them achieve recently or reminisce about a fun memory you shared together. This helps break the ice and shows that you genuinely remember them: "Hey Lisa, I noticed you recently celebrated your fifth anniversary at XYZ company – that's awesome! Congrats!"

H – Honesty: Just be upfront about it, seriously. Mention that it's been a while and share why you wanted to get back in touch. This touch of honesty not only clears the air but also shows that you're genuinely interested in rekindling the connection and demonstrates vulnerability: "I know it's been a while since our last chat back at the entrepreneur meetup. I've been thinking about our conversation about morning rituals as I've been waking up earlier to journal like you suggested!"

A – Ask: Ask a specific question or bring up a topic that's of interest to them based on your prior interaction(s). Maybe ask about any exciting projects they've been working on or get their take on a hot topic in your industry. This not only revs up the chat but also gives it some direction, making it easier for them to jump back into the conversation with you: "I would love to hear your thoughts on this new study that shows the impact of morning routines on daily productivity. Can I send you the link? No rush, just curious to hear your perspective!"

T – Thankfulness: End your message by saying thanks. This not only shows that you truly appreciate their time in reading your message but also sets a respectful tone that will make them more likely to respond: "Thanks for taking the time to read this. I know you're a busy gal making moves! I really appreciate it and hope we can reconnect soon. Have a great week!"

Remember, the other person may not respond, and that's okay. Focus on the little things that are within control while networking and keep your head up! Just keep reaching out, keep engaging, and most importantly, keep being you, social anxiety and all. There's a whole world of opportunities out there, and your next big break might just be a message away.

LinkedIn Groups

If you prefer small or big group settings for networking over one-on-one private messages, LinkedIn groups may be just the thing for you. These groups offer a structured space where you can engage at your own pace, find people who share your interests and goals, and slowly build your networking muscles in a low-pressure environment.

With thousands of groups to choose from, how do you find the right ones to join? Again, it all comes down to what your networking goals are. Picking the right group is all about knowing what you're looking for and why. Are you hunting for career advice, looking to share industry insights and stay up to date on the latest news, or looking for a community that can support you as you grow? Your goals should guide your choice.

There are essentially three different "types" of groups on LinkedIn: Professional Growth Groups, Career and Opportunity Groups, and Community Groups.

Professional Growth Groups are awesome for keeping up-to-date or leveling up in your field. These communities offer a treasure trove of resources, discussions, and expert advice. They're ideal for staying ahead in your career, learning new techniques or skills, or even switching industries. Example: Digital Marketing Professionals, 2 million members.

Career and Opportunity Groups are great if you're looking for your next job or for more career opportunities. This type of group provides a platform for discovering job openings, connecting with potential employers, and networking across industries. They're also great for finding mentors and expanding your LinkedIn network beyond your immediate circle. Example: Technology Jobs Network – #1 IT Careers Group, 132k members.

Community Groups are perfect for networking on a more personal level, because you already have something in common with other members. This type of group includes alumni groups, interest-based groups, and local/regional groups. These are perfect for fostering relationships based on shared educational backgrounds, common interests, or being from the same hood. Whether you're looking to catch up with old classmates, get geeky with niche topics, or meet other professionals nearby, these groups make it easy to find your people. Example: Network After Work – Seattle Business/Professional Networking Events, 5k members.

To find groups on LinkedIn, simply type in your keyword(s) in the search bar at the top of your LinkedIn mobile or desktop app, and then click on groups to see a full list of groups that include the keyword(s).

Here are some quick tips to help you make the most of your time in the groups that you decide to join:

- **Start small:** It can be overwhelming – especially in groups like some of the examples above that include hundreds of thousands or even millions of people worldwide – to just jump into the conversation. Scroll through the posts to get a better idea of the rules and types of content that people expect and start liking and commenting on some of the content that you find interesting.
- **Curate and share:** Start saving content that matches the interests of the group and that you think will be valuable to other members, like exciting news within your industry, community events, or interesting blogs about the group topic. Start sharing some things that you're genuinely excited about and invite conversation by asking for opinions or thoughts.
- **Be a team player:** Consistency is key. Try to contribute regularly to keep building connections and reinforcing your presence in the group. Also, if the group hosts virtual events or meetups, attending these can be a great way to connect more deeply with members beyond just the group feed.

With the right groups, you can transform your career, learn from others, share your expertise, and maybe even step outside of your comfort zone just a bit. Remember, everyone in these groups started somewhere, just like you. Whether you're in a giant group like Digital Marketing Professionals or a cozy online club like Network After Work – Seattle, the key is to engage in ways that feel right for you.

LinkedIn Events

LinkedIn Events provide an easy way to dip your toes into networking. Whether it's a casual audio event or an in-the-moment LinkedIn Live, these events can be a goldmine for connections and learning, all while wearing your favorite pair of sweatpants.

There are four types of LinkedIn events currently available: LinkedIn Audio Events, LinkedIn Live, in person, and third-party virtual. We've discussed webinars before and we'll dig in deeper into face-to-face meetups in the next chapter, so for now I want to focus our attention on LinkedIn Audio Events and LinkedIn Live.

LinkedIn Audio Events: Think of these as your favorite podcast, but interactive. You can listen in, ask questions, or even contribute to the discussion without having to worry about what your hair looks like. It's a fun way to engage with speakers and participants in a real-time audio-only setting. I've hosted a few of these, and they are one of my favorite ways to network without worrying about if you're averting your eyes too often, or if the other person can notice you fidgeting with your hair. These are a great "low-impact" networking option, whether you are hosting or attending.

LinkedIn Live: This is where the action happens live and directly in people's LinkedIn feed. Imagine tuning into a broadcast where you can comment and interact, not just with the hosts but also with other viewers. It's like being at a conference or a panel discussion, except you can do it while sipping coffee at your kitchen table! LinkedIn Live sessions often cover everything from industry trends and tutorials to Q&A sessions and panel discussions. They may feel a bit more intimidating than audio events, but they're a great way to get noticed, make new connections, and even pick up some valuable tips along the way.

Now, because you're spending so much time and energy finding and registering for these events, you want to make sure that you absolutely make it worth your while. Here are some tips for what to do before, during, and after both LinkedIn Audio Events and LinkedIn Live video events:

Before the Event

Prep ahead: Do a little homework. If you're attending a LinkedIn Live or Audio Event, check out the topics and speakers in advance. Make sure that not only is the topic of interest to you but also that the speaker(s) have the experience or expertise to host a valuable event. Doing a little bit of research will also help you to think of a few questions to ask.

Check your tech: If there's one thing I've learned as a virtual speaker and remote instructor for LinkedIn Learning, it's that technology will fail. Something that has been working fine will suddenly develop a fickle attitude right before you need it to perform properly. Set aside time for those inevitable glitches. Make sure your internet connection is stable, and your LinkedIn app or website is up to date to avoid any problems during the event.

During the Event
Be an active participant: One thing that I've noticed when speaking specifically to students is that they listen passively. It can become easy to treat online events as lectures where you can just exist in the background. So, make a conscious effort to be active. Don't be shy to use the chat feature. Remember, your comments can be seen by other attendees and speakers, which is a fantastic way to make connections and connect with them post-event.

Stay relaxed: I recognize that social anxiety exists on a spectrum, and even online events can feel scary. It's okay if it's hard; give yourself grace and remember that progress doesn't need to happen only in giant leaps. Also remember that you're in your comfort zone (home), so keep a beverage or snacks at hand, and try to enjoy the session as much as you can.

After the event
Follow up: If someone's comments or insights caught your attention during the event, reach out with a personalized connection request. Time is of the essence. I love getting connection requests the same day as the virtual event because I have immediate context.

Share the love: I cannot stress this enough. Posting your positive experience at an event publicly is a super-effective way to create a good impression on the people involved in it. Post a LinkedIn update about your key takeaways from the event. Tag speakers or participants if relevant. This not only shows your engagement but also boosts your visibility as well!

Bank it in your networking journal: Take a moment to think about whether your experience with the event was a positive or negative one. If you felt great after the event, look for other similar events to attend and keep attending. If it was a negative experience, consider why it felt that way. Was it the speaker? The format? The number of attendees? Reflecting on each networking experience, both on and offline, is so important to create a schedule that works best for you.

LinkedIn Content

Some of the best networking I've ever done has not been in a crowded room; it's been through content that I created on LinkedIn. If we think of LinkedIn as the world's largest networking event, then I want you to also think of your LinkedIn content as your handshake. With the right strategy and copywriting skills, your content can act as a friendly introduction and a spark for engaging conversations. Picture each post you put out there as your way of reaching through the screen and offering a handshake, a smile, and an invitation into your community.

There are so many different types of content that you can create on LinkedIn that it can quickly get overwhelming. It can be as tricky as ordering coffee at that fancy new cafe around the corner. Do you want a classic Americano post, a sweet and frothy delectable video, or just a quick espresso shot of a poll? Let me break these down for you so you can decide which one best suits your skills and goals for networking on LinkedIn.

Text and Photo Posts

I'm a firm believer that people don't care about what you offer until they know two things:

1. Who you are and what you stand for
2. That you understand them

So often, people look at creating content on LinkedIn as a frivolous activity that isn't necessary when it comes to growing in your career or networking, but imagine this:

> *You walk into a networking event at a local co-working space, feeling a mix of excitement and nerves. You spot the person you've been eager to meet. Without a second thought, you stride across the room and tap them on the shoulder from behind. As they turn around, their expression one of slight confusion, and you jump straight in.*

> *With a wide grin, you blurt out, "I help brands, businesses, and ambitious people leverage the power of LinkedIn! Here's my business card. Call me!" Before they can even respond, you hand them your card, turn on your heels, and dart off to repeat the process with someone else.*
>
> *The person is left standing there, still trying to place your face, slightly bewildered and holding your business card. They're unsure of who you are, what you actually do, or why they should even call you.*

Now consider this. If you were that person being handed the business card, how would that interaction make you feel? What are the chances that you'd put it in your pocket and call the next day?

My point here is that without establishing a connection that feels genuine and authentic, simply distributing business cards like you're dealing out a deck of cards at a poker table won't cut it.

LinkedIn content can bridge the gap and help to foster relationships online so that you're rarely walking into a room cold. Imagine this scenario, after spending some time creating content on LinkedIn:

> *Instead of a hasty introduction at a networking event and getting zero calls or emails afterward, you have been sharing thoughtful, engaging text and photo posts on LinkedIn.*
>
> *These posts reflect your expertise, sure, but also demonstrate your personal values. Over time, you've woven a narrative about who you are, what you stand for, and how deeply you understand the challenges and core values of the people around you.*
>
> *One day, you attend the same networking event. You don't have to introduce yourself from scratch because your posts have already made the rounds. People recognize you, not just from your profile picture but from the stories you've shared. They feel like they already kind of know you. When you approach that person you've been eager to meet, they greet you with a smile, saying, "Oh hey! Michaela! I loved your latest post on LinkedIn. It really resonated with me!"*

This is the power of content on LinkedIn. It's not frivolous; it's foundational. It creates familiarity and trust before you step into the room. By the time you hand over your business card, it won't just be an introduction – it'll be a reconnection, and that's a powerful shift, don't you think? So, let's get into it!

Crafting Stories That Connect

Here's a weird little secret for you. When I create written content, before I press post or publish, I ask myself, "Does this have enough strawberry jelly?"

When I was a little girl, I hated taking pills so much that I would run away and hide in closets (sorry, Mom). So, one day, my mom decided to hide a pill in a spoonful of strawberry jelly and feed it to me. And, surprisingly, it worked! Suddenly, my irrational fear of choking on a pill subsided in the sweet, gelatinous deliciousness.

What does that have to do with writing or networking? Well, just like that sneaky spoonful of jelly made the medicine go down easier, I use the same principle in my writing. In other words, have I added enough relatable, genuine storytelling to turn my message into something palatable? It's all about making sure my LinkedIn content is as approachable and engaging as a chat with an old friend over coffee.

This little check ensures that I'm not just dumping information or broadcasting another freaking tutorial or "here's how you need to do things!" into the digital void. Instead, I'm crafting something that feels personal, something that offers a taste of who I am, and in turn gives people permission to share a bit of themselves too. Because, let's face it, whether it's in the newsfeed of LinkedIn or the bustling crowd of a networking event, people want real connections. Don't you? And if I can make my text and photo posts as delightful as a spoonful of strawberry jelly? Well, then I've found a way to make meaningful connections that stick, figuratively speaking!

Nailing Your Text and Photo Post with My Copywriting Formula

Copywriting on LinkedIn for me was such a struggle, until I realized that there was a way to format my posts to maximize my impact. Here's my handy copywriting formula that has helped me to create and share many viral posts on LinkedIn since 2016!

What (your story): Begin with a vivid description of an event or personal experience. For example, earlier I shared a story about how I hated pills as a little girl. This narrative should be super detailed and emotional, making it easy for your audience to visualize and connect with the story.

So what (the lessons): Now you want to share why your story matters for the person reading it. Unpack it a bit. What's the takeaway? Share a nugget of wisdom or lessons learned that add value for the reader.

Now what (call to action): Wrap up with an invitation for a chat, a question that begs a comment, or whatever you want the reader to do next. It's all about keeping the conversation going and providing direction for them.

Opening with a Scroll Stopper

Your first line should grab attention like the smell of fresh coffee in the morning. Start with a cliffhanger or a punchy quote that makes scrolling past impossible. It's your hook that draws people into the story you're about to tell. For example, when I started this section, I opened with "Here's a weird little secret for you: when I create written content, before I press post or publish, I ask myself 'Does this have enough strawberry jelly?'"

Choosing the Right Photo (If You Include One)

The photo you choose should do more than just look good; it should tell part of the story. If you're talking about a breakthrough moment, why not show where it happened? Use it to help set the scene and deepen the impact of your words.

For example, for the strawberry jelly story, I might use a photo of me eating a spoonful of jelly, or one of me running away from a bottle of pills. Don't be afraid to get creative and be playful. Having a lighthearted sense of humor won't make people respect you less!

With these tips, your LinkedIn posts can become a delightful blend of personal touch and professional tips, making the networking scene a little more chill, especially those of us who find the usual hustle a bit overwhelming.

Newsletters

Think of a LinkedIn newsletter like your personal broadcast channel. It's a direct way to drop your latest thoughts and stories right into your followers' inboxes off of LinkedIn, and into their newsfeed. Unlike posts, with their 3,000-character limit, you can write to your heart's content with newsletters, which allow 100,000 characters or 10,000 words.

Newsletters are a powerful tool for building thought leadership and fostering personal connections, but they are also a great option for those with social anxiety. First, you control the interaction. When you create a newsletter on LinkedIn, you choose the cadence of publishing (daily, weekly, biweekly, monthly). You get to share when you are ready and are feeling up to it, which can help to ease nerves and take off some pressure. Having a consistent presence can also help you to foster and build relationships without always having to show up at events or engage in real time conversations.

From a strategic perspective, newsletters are great because they go directly to your subscribers, where other content only hits the newsfeed of your connections. This is super handy because many people who may want to hear from you might not be on LinkedIn on a daily or even weekly basis, so this helps you to reach them where they are more likely to be hanging out during their workday: their email inbox.

Polls

Polls on LinkedIn are the ultimate icebreaker, especially when networking feels a bit daunting. Imagine you're at a large conference lunch table, not sure about how to initiate a conversation. Dropping a quick, interesting question to the group can get people talking, and that's exactly what polls do on LinkedIn.

They are light, easy-to-create interactions that invite others to share their opinions without requiring much effort. You can ask something like "Do you think AI-generated headshots belong on LinkedIn?" and people vote. They feel involved, and you get to interact in a meaningful way without the pressure of a direct conversation.

Polls can also allow you to gauge interest and opinions and understand the pulse of your audience. This information can be incredibly useful for the next time that you create content, so that you are catering what you create to what your audience actually wants.

Videos

Videos bring your personality front and center, making it way easier for people to see and get to know the real you. It's like a virtual handshake, but better, because you can script it, rehearse, and edit until it feels just right, which is perfect for easing those networking jitters.

While video can be a powerful tool to connect with your audience, I realize that it's easier said than done when it comes to battling social anxiety. Video feels more intimidating for many who prefer to work and create behind the scenes.

My first videos were a disaster. I would break out in nervous hives up to my earlobes. In fact, it still happens from time to time when I'm doing video interviews or virtual speaking gigs. Here are some things that I've discovered through the process of learning to create video content as a socially anxious gal:

- **Start small:** You don't have to jump right into creating an hour-long video from the start! When I was struggling in the beginning, instead of diving right into longer videos for LinkedIn, I used Instagram Stories. Each story was only 15 seconds, and I thought, "Okay, I can definitely handle 15 seconds!" I did one story, then another, and soon enough it started to feel easy and natural to create multiple stories during my day.
- **Use a teleprompter:** Some people are amazing at just pulling out their phone, recording a video, and then moving on with their day. I am not that person. I have to do multiple takes, I inevitably mess up my words, and if I have no script, I'm almost certain to go off on a tangent. That's why when it comes to creating more polished videos for LinkedIn, I use a teleprompter app for my phone like BigVu, which overlays the script on your camera so that it looks like you are speaking directly to your audience.
- **Create a cozy environment:** I make sure my recording space is comfortable and reflects a setting that I feel comfortable in. Whether it's adding plants, books, or art to make the space feel calming, or just ensuring it's quiet and free from interruptions, a familiar environment can really help you feel more at ease when you press record.

Curated Content

If the idea of trying to come up with something enlightening or interesting to share consistently on LinkedIn is making your head spin, think of curated content as your secret weapon for keeping your LinkedIn bumpin' without the sweat of creating something new every time. Your job is to just sift through the sea of information out there and pick gems that sparkle just right for your network.

You can sign up for an account for an RSS aggregator like Feedly to keep tabs on your favorite topics, or follow thought leaders in your industry on LinkedIn, and when you find a resource that you think is beneficial for your audience, share it on your profile with a personal twist.

Add a quick comment on why you find it valuable or ask a question to encourage interaction. This not only shows that you're up-to-date with current trends but also invites your followers to contribute their thoughts, turning a simple share into a conversation starter.

Why You Absolutely Need a LinkedIn Content Strategy for Networking

Sometimes when I say the word "strategy," it conjures up images of that over-cologned sales guy flashing a too-wide grin and pushing a hard sell. But I promise you, a content strategy for LinkedIn is nothing like that. It's not about aggressive tactics or slick pitches. Instead, it's about thoughtful planning that will maximize your time and effort.

Think of a content strategy as your roadmap for LinkedIn networking. It clearly defines what you'll post, when you'll post it, and why it's relevant. This structured approach is key to more effective networking because you're consistently engaging with your LinkedIn connections in meaningful ways. By having a plan, you avoid that last-minute "WTF am I going to post on LinkedIn this week?" dread and can focus more on interacting with your connections instead of scrambling to hit publish or feeling overwhelmed.

So, without further ado, here's your step-by-step roadmap to creating kickass LinkedIn content that will help you grow your network:

> **Step 1: Define your goals.** Pinpoint exactly what you want to achieve on LinkedIn. What does success look like to you? Are you looking to expand your network, land new opportunities, or establish yourself as an industry thought leader? Setting clear goals will steer your content strategy in the right direction.
>
> **Step 2: Understand your people.** Get to know the people you want to connect with. What are their interests, needs, and challenges? Understanding your audience is crucial for creating content that resonates.

Step 3: Plan your content mix. Decide on the types of content you'll share. There isn't a right or wrong format of content, although the algorithm may favor one format over another from time to time. Focus instead on which format feels like the most natural fit for your skills and schedule. If you enjoy writing, don't feel pressured to create dancing videos, and if you prefer to be on camera, go all in on videos that allow your creativity to flow! The key here is to choose formats that don't feel like a chore; creating content should be fun.

Step 4: Create a schedule. Create a posting schedule that works for you – daily, weekly, biweekly, or even monthly. Consistency keeps you visible and top of mind with your connections, but choose a cadence that feels sustainable. Posting a monthly newsletter and spending the rest of your time interacting with connections and answering messages is more impactful than posting daily if you can only handle doing it for two weeks before you get burnt out. Personally, I post about once a week on both my company page and personal profile. In some seasons, I may post more frequently, but in the one I'm in right now, weekly content works best.

Step 5: Batch your content. Like meal prepping for the week, set aside time to create and either put together a document with topics and bullet points you want to cover in upcoming content, or schedule posts in advance. This helps to minimize daily pressure and to manage any social anxiety related to constant content creation because you know what's coming up. I like to do this on Fridays so that I have the weekend to let ideas simmer and mentally prepare for the week ahead.

Step 6: Don't post and ghost. True networking is about interaction. Make sure to engage with the comments on your posts and participate in the comment section of other peoples' posts. This builds stronger relationships more naturally.

Step 7: Review and adjust. Step aside time each month (or biweekly) to review the performance of your posts to understand what works and what doesn't. Use this data to refine your strategy and improve your content over time.

One pro tip is to look beyond just the analytics on your posts and check out the comments section. This can be a treasure trove of information to find out what's resonating most with your audience and maybe dig in a bit deeper on specific topics. By following these steps, you create a structured yet flexible content strategy that enhances your LinkedIn networking without the stress-related procrastination!

LinkedIn Recommendations

LinkedIn recommendations are personal testimonials from colleagues, clients, or employers who validate your professional capabilities. They're more detailed and personal than simple skill endorsements and are like personal shout-outs from people who've worked closely with you.

LinkedIn recommendations are like gold for your profile, and especially so with social anxiety because they can boost your confidence and credibility while strengthening your relationships. Also, asking for recommendations isn't an easy task! If the root of your social anxiety is a fear of rejection, one way to practice becoming more "rejection proof" is by putting yourself out there and asking for those who know you best to vouch for you. Once you get into the swing of it, it'll become easier and easier to reach out to your broader circle.

How to Ask for Recommendations

Reach out to the right people: Focus on people who are really in your corner, like a former supervisor who promoted you or clients who've seen your magic and referred others to you. They're your best bet for impactful, glowing recommendations.

Make it easy: Help your recommenders by sharing specific achievements or skills you'd love them to highlight. You could even draft up a few points for them if they're super short on time. This makes their job easier and ensures the recommendation really sings your praises.

Make it personal: Skip the impersonal LinkedIn prompt, and don't just send the request via LinkedIn. Reach out with a friendly note through your usual channels like email or a quick call – however you normally communicate with this person. This personal nudge not only shows that you truly value their endorsement but also keeps your request on their radar.

Share your why: Let them know why their recommendation is so important for you. Understanding how their words can boost your career can inspire them to craft a recommendation that really counts and comes straight from the heart.

Writing Awesome Recommendations

Focus on the details: When you're writing recommendations, get super specific with concrete examples. Did they pull off a creative solution under tight deadlines? Were they the go-to problem-solver in the office? Spotlight these specific instances where they went beyond the call of duty. Not only will it help them look good, but it also will show your requester that you remember their contributor and appreciate them.

Follow up: After you've written that glowing recommendation, send them a quick message. Let them know you've put in a good word for them. It's a thoughtful final step that wraps things up nicely and keeps the lines of communication open to continue the conversation. Plus, it often activates the desire to reciprocate, so be open to sharing where you need help in return to keep the good vibes flowing.

Before we move on after navigating the sometimes choppy waters of LinkedIn, I want to take a minute to get real with you. As someone who once struggled deeply with agoraphobia, I can't stress enough how life changing this platform has been for me. LinkedIn wasn't just a tool; it became my lifeline, connecting me to people who pulled me up and who, to this day, are cheering me on from the sidelines. It allowed me to finally forge a career path on my own terms, from the comfort of home, slowly breaking down the walls of my social anxiety.

If you're feeling stuck or like you can't achieve your dreams because you are wired a bit differently, know that LinkedIn can help you grow in ways you might not think possible until you see it for yourself. It's more than a network; it's a community where you can grow at your own pace, find your tribe, and even share your story to inspire others.

So take the first step, however small. I'm stoked to hear how everything turns out for you!

Networking Beyond LinkedIn: Understanding Audiences and Building a Consistent Personal Brand

LinkedIn is essentially the corner office of social media. It's professional, more polished, and people are there to learn, grow, and connect while doing it. But what about the rest of the social media platforms? Each platform offers unique opportunities to expand your network in a more personal way.

Knowing Your Audience

The first step in networking on any social media platform is to understand who your audience is. Each attracts a different demographic and has its own culture and unspoken rules.

- **LinkedIn:** Think of it as your office: neat, professional, and a bit on the formal side. You can loosen up a bit, I promise, but also keep it classy. Save the slang and spicy language for other spots, because polls I've done on here show that LinkedIn users are not a fan of cursing in content and messages. This is your stage to share your challenges, celebrate your champagne moments, and interact and engage like you would at an in-person networking event.

- **Instagram:** Picture it as your favorite little coffee shop where you network over coffee with friends. It's more relaxed than LinkedIn and visually engaging. While networking here, you might chat about a successful meeting, but then switch gears to share an Instagram Story of you browsing through racks at a local thrift shop. Some choose to focus on business, some focus more on personal; it's up to you which route to take, but remember that people here want to see a more candid, real side of you.

   What I love about Instagram for networking is that especially when your content leans more personal, it feels more spontaneous when you chat in the DMs and a work opportunity pops up. This can be particularly helpful for those with social anxiety who feel icky in environments where more transactional networking takes place.

- **Facebook:** This is like the backyard BBQ where the whole community shows up, from old classmates to former coworkers, and even distant relatives. It's laid back and welcoming, but with so many different types of people around, it can also feel a bit overwhelming at times. For those with social anxiety, this wide assortment of people can seem scary, but it's also a space where you can engage at your own pace. You can join groups with people who have similar interests, spend more time messaging one-on-one, or devote your time to posting and engaging in the comment section. If you don't know exactly where to start networking online, Facebook is an easy starting point to get into a socializing groove.

There's no "right" place to network online; you can make new connections on so many different, ever-changing platforms. The key is to find a spot on the internet that feels like it fits your vibe and who you want to meet.

Whether it's setting up Zoom calls with the professional crowd on LinkedIn, swapping recipes on Instagram, joining the rapid fire exchanges on X, or diving into in-depth discussions in subreddits on Reddit, each platform offers a unique flavor of interaction. It's up to you to discover which one fits you best in your networking journey. So start exploring, and don't be afraid to try new platforms. You never know where your next great connection will come from; I sure didn't!

Creating a Consistent Personal Brand on Social Media

Crafting a personal brand on social media isn't just about selling or influencing; it can be a lifeline for those of us navigating the networking world with social anxiety. One of the first steps I was able to take while overcoming agoraphobia was reaching out to friends on Facebook and having candid conversations about what had been going on. Learning how to interact with others online eventually gave me the courage to foster those relationships offline as well.

The key with networking on social media is to make sure that the online you and the offline you are consistent, that whatever you are presenting on Instagram or LinkedIn is what people can expect from you in person. Your tone and voice across platforms should be steady and genuine. This consistency not only helps lessen the anxiety of wondering how you're coming off but also builds trust and makes connections feel more natural.

Embrace this authentic approach and let your true self shine through in every post, comment, and message. This authenticity invites others into your world, making it easier to engage in meaningful conversations that could, and often do, lead to real world connections. Remember, every interaction is a step toward building a community where you feel at home, both online and off. It's about creating a cozy corner online where you can be your true self, encouraging others to do the same, and slowly bridging the gap between your digital persona and the real you.

Handling Negative Interactions

I'll never forget those first negative comments. A post I shared on LinkedIn somehow went viral, racking up views like crazy. Initially, it was thrilling.

The post was hitting just my LinkedIn connections – a few hundred people who actually knew me. The comments were all cheers and high-fives: "Congratulations on your new gig, Mick!" "Wow, what a cool story, can't wait to see what you do next!" "I always knew you had it in you."

I was flying high, basking in the warmth of their words. But as the post spread beyond my immediate circle, reaching friends of friends of friends, the tone started to change. Suddenly, I was seeing comments like "Maybe spend less time posting on LinkedIn and more time fixing your makeup." "Your last job only lasted a few months, I'm sure this one will go well LOL." "And who are you? Why would I care?"

That's when my bubble burst. Critiques on my looks, my job history… it all came flooding in. Honestly, it knocked the wind out of me and I cried that day.

But then the next day I took a deep breath and remembered something important, a quote from Teddy Roosevelt that Brené Brown highlights in her book *Daring Greatly*. She talks about the courage it takes to "show up and be seen," to step into the arena even when you can't predict or control the outcome.[1] Roosevelt put it like this:

> "It is not the critic who counts; not the man who points out how the strong man stumbles, or where the doer of deeds could have done them better. The credit belongs to the man who is actually marred by dust and sweat and blood; who strives valiantly; who errs, who comes short again and again, because there is no effort without error and shortcoming; but who does actually strive to do the deeds; who knows great enthusiasms, the great devotions; who spends himself in a worthy cause; and who at the worst, if he fails, at least fails while daring greatly."[2]

That's the moment I decided I wasn't going to let the critics knock me down. Sure, the negative comments kept coming, but they began to feel more like stubbing my toe; they stung for a moment but then I'd move on. I kept posting, kept engaging, and slowly those harsh words lost some of their power.

It's easy to feel beaten down by the negativity; in fact, if you told me before I started posting what some people would say about me, I probably wouldn't have had the courage to publish. But here's the thing: people will always have opinions about you, no matter what. Networking and interacting online is about stepping into the arena, where the real action happens, not sitting safely on the sidelines.

The key to handling negative feedback online is about taking a deep breath, leaning into the vulnerability, and remembering why you started sharing in the first place.

Constructive Criticism versus Trolling

When you engage on social media, no matter the platform, you're likely to bump into all kinds of feedback. Some of it may be welcome and helpful once you take a step back and really think about it, and some of it is as unwelcome as decaf coffee when you need a double espresso. Here's how to tell the difference between trolling, which is just noise you might want to tune out, and constructive criticism, which can help you grow.

Trolling

Trolling is when people jump into online conversations just to cause trouble; there are no good intentions involved. They're not there to contribute or offer constructive feedback; they just want to stir shit up.

Trolling can range anywhere from mildly annoying comments to outright nasty online abuse. The main goal is to disrupt and make you feel bad. Recognizing trolling for what it is can help you stay focused on the positive interactions and keep your online space supportive and fun.

Here's an example of trolling. You've just shared a post on LinkedIn about a recent success you're really proud of. Maybe you've just completed a big project, or you've been invited to speak at an upcoming conference. The responses start off great! Your connections are congratulating you, sharing in your excitement, and offering words of encouragement. It feels amazing! Then, out of nowhere, a comment pops up: "Oh great, another wannabe expert. How about you try getting a real job?" Ouch. That stings, and it's completely uncalled for. Before you know it, a few more trolls jump in with comments like "Why should anyone listen to you?" and "Wow, this is just embarrassing."

Suddenly, your joy is overshadowed by these awful comments. It's important to remember that these trolls aren't interested in meaningful dialogue or your achievements; they just want to make you doubt yourself.

Constructive Criticism

Constructive criticism is meant to challenge you but in a good way. It's specific, actionable, and the goal is helping you improve. When someone offers constructive criticism, they're usually respectful and focus on what you can do better. They aren't just dumping on what you did wrong.

Initially, constructive criticism may sting (I love the meme that says, "When I say constructive criticism I really mean compliment me"), but eventually you'll feel empowered with new knowledge that can help you to improve. Here are a couple of examples of constructive criticism:

Feedback: "I loved how engaging your presentation was! If you could make the conclusion as snappy as your intro, you'd crush it!"

Feedback: "You're a great writer, and this article is shaping up really well. It might be helpful to watch out for run-on sentences to make your arguments as clear as possible to the reader."

Recognizing Constructive Criticism: RISE When it comes to giving and recognizing constructive criticism, think RISE: Respectful, Insightful, Supportive, and Encouraging. Here's how it breaks down:

Respectful: Constructive criticism is delivered with respect. It's all about a gentle tone, focusing on the task, and staying positive and specific. For example, instead of saying, "You're not good at presentations," a respectful approach would be "Your presentation was engaging, but using more visuals could make your key points clearer." It's all about helping, not hurting.

Insightful: Good feedback offers new perspectives and insights, leading to those aha moments. It helps you see your work in a new light, like "I noticed your approach here; have you considered this method? It might help streamline your process." This way, you're not just pointing out what's wrong, but also showing a path forward.

Supportive: Constructive criticism feels like a hug, not a punch. It's meant to help you develop your skills, not just point out flaws. For instance, "Your writing style is unique and engaging; tightening up a few sections could make your message even more powerful." Supportive feedback shows you care about their growth.

Encouraging: Finally, constructive feedback should leave you feeling motivated and positive. It points out areas for improvement but in a way that encourages you, like "You're on the right track with your project; a bit more focus on the data could really elevate your work to the next level." It keeps the positive vibes going.

Using the RISE formula helps you not only receive and give effective feedback but also creates a positive, productive environment where everyone can grow and improve.

Handling Negative Comments Online as a No Fear Networker

Before you hit that reply button, make sure that you know which type of feedback you're responding to. Is it constructive criticism, or trolling?

For constructive criticism, here's what to do next:

- **Acknowledge the feedback:** Start by recognizing the feedback. Show appreciation for the person's time and effort. Example: "Hey [person's name], thanks for the feedback! I appreciate you taking the time to help me improve."
- **Stay calm and keep cool:** Try and view the criticism as a chance to grow. Focus on the constructive aspect. If you're seeing red and your ego is throwing a tantrum, take some time until you're ready. It's okay to feel taken aback; feedback is hard, even if it's constructive. Sometimes I'll take a walk outside or sleep on it before responding so that I make sure I'm addressing it with a clear mind. Example: "I see your point about [specific aspect]."
- **Ask for clarity:** If something in the feedback isn't clear, don't hesitate to ask for more details. You want to make sure that you understand fully before responding. Example: "Could you tell me a bit more about what you mean by [specific issue]? I want to make sure I understand."
- **Share next steps:** If the constructive criticism is valuable after reflection, make sure to let the person know the actions you're going to take in your reply. Only do this if you mean it! Example: "I'm going to look into that. I haven't thought about it that way before."

- **Keep it positive and end on a positive note:** Remember that constructive criticism is also hard to give, and the person on the other end is likely sharing it because they care about your success. Keep the vibes upbeat and end on a positive note. Example: "I really do appreciate you taking the time to check out my work and sharing some advice. I'm looking forward to implementing these tips!"

Now, here's how to respond to trolling:

- **Take a deep breath:** Remember that negative information can flood and activate parts of your brain and create an emotional response. Taking a few deep breaths can help calm your nervous system so that you can handle responding promptly.
- **Set firm boundaries:** Remember that this is your cozy corner of the internet. If a house guest barged into your house and started making a mess, you'd either tell them to clean up or ask them to leave. The same is true for unkind responses or trolling. You want to set the precedent that that behavior won't be tolerated. Example: "Hey, let's keep it constructive and respectful, please."
- **Clean it up:** If the person agrees to respect your boundaries, moderate the comments to make sure that they're truly complying and that other users don't jump in (trolling can be contagious). If necessary, use the platform's tools to block and report, and delete comments. It is not your job to try and convince people to be kind.
- **Remember your worth:** Always keep in mind Eleanor Roosevelt's wise words, "No one can make you feel inferior without your consent." Don't let trolls shake your confidence or derail you from your goals.

By handling negative comments with confidence and a clear strategy, you not only protect your space but also set a powerful example for your audience. It's not so much what is said, but how you handle it that truly matters. People are watching for your reaction, so let your response reflect the no fear networker that I know you are.

8 | Face-to-Face Networking Without Fear

Alright, let's switch gears from our cozy couch sessions to stepping out into the real world to (gulp) meet people during face-to-face networking! Whether the mere thought makes you want to sprint in the opposite direction or just gives you a few butterflies, fear not. This chapter is all about rocking the hell out of those real-world meetups (or at least not hiding in the bathroom the entire time). We're going to unpack some top tips that'll have you mingling like a pro, feeling less like you're in a room full of strangers, and more like you're just meeting friends you haven't made yet. Ready? Take a deep breath and let's get into it.

Strategies for Joining Conversations

One of the biggest challenges people tend to have when it comes to networking is figuring out how to enter a conversation. In Chapter 6, we covered conversation starters that won't make you cringe, and those work great for individuals and one-on-one chats. But what about the step before that, when you enter a room, look around, and see a group of people huddled together in conversation? You're on the outside of the circle and you don't know who to approach or how to join in.

According to communication expert Bruce Lambert, there is a simple way to approach this.[1] When someone finishes speaking, they might pause and continue if no one else jumps in, they could pass the mic to someone else, or another person might take the initiative to start speaking, which is a process known as "self-selecting."

So if you're looking to join the fray, remember that bulldozing into the conversation is a big no-no. That's like cutting in line at the coffee shop – definitely not cool. Bruce suggests a smoother move: simply wait for a moment of silence, then confidently self-select and share your thoughts. It's that easy!

And just like that, you're not just on the outside looking in. You're right there in the thick of it, ready to mingle and make those connections count.

Fine-Tuning Your First Impression with Charisma

When I first started networking, both in person and online, one of the hardest things for me to overcome was that I felt so nervous. I would get so in my head worrying that people could see my social anxiety on the outside that it actually increased my social anxiety to the point where it ran the show.

I often looked in awe at others who seemed to network and communicate with such ease, wondering how they not only seemed confident but also made the person or people they were speaking with feel so comfortable too. Maybe you know someone like that in your own life!

According to Vanessa Van Edwards, a bestselling author, researcher, and founder of the behavior lab Science of People, this is called charisma. Charisma is a combination of both warmth and competence. But what's really cool is that charisma can be learned![2] Vanessa points out that charisma can be enhanced through simple nonverbal cues that signal both warmth and competence. For example, think about the way you make eye contact, how you use your hands when you talk, or even raising or furrowing your eyebrows. These might seem like small tweaks, but they can significantly impact how people perceive you.

One tip from Vanessa that really resonated with me is the power of visible hands. Showing your hands during conversations, especially at the very beginning, acts as a subtle cue of honesty and openness. It's like saying, "I have nothing to hide," which helps build trust effortlessly.

Another powerful tool? The eyebrow flash. This quick lift of your eyebrows when you first meet someone or begin speaking to them serves as a nonverbal "hey," signaling openness and recognition, making others feel seen and immediately welcomed.

And lastly, charisma can be communicated through your vocal tone. Instead of letting nerves pitch your voice higher and sounding a little like Elmo, take a breath and speak from your chest. This produces a tone that's not only calming but asserts a quiet confidence, and also signals competence because it sounds certain, instead of like a question.

So next time you're at an event or meet someone new, remember these cues. Start with visible hands, manage your vocal tone, and perhaps give a quick eyebrow flash. These subtle signals can help set the stage for a lasting first impression.

Overcoming Awkward Moments

When I was about 12, I attended a track-and-field summer camp. One memorable day, we were all psyched for an obstacle course race. I was in full sprint mode, sailing over a hurdle, when suddenly the world got a whole lot cooler – literally. I glanced down and, to my horror, realized that my new tearaway pants had done just that: torn away. They lay in a crumpled heap on the brick-red synthetic track.

There I was, the center of attention, in my faded purple dot undies, surrounded by a sea of wide-eyed peers. Most days from that time are a blur, but ask me about that moment of epic embarrassment? I could run through every mortifying detail like it was just yesterday.

Maybe you don't have a story quite as embarrassing as standing in your undies, but let's be real: awkward moments are just part of the deal when you're mixing it up with other humans. Whether it's tripping up the stairs, spilling coffee on your shirt right before a client meeting, or accidentally calling your boss "mom," these cringeworthy snippets are unavoidable.

So instead of praying that they never happen (which is, of course, plan A here), let's talk about ways to overcome those common awkward moments during conversations that are bound to happen sooner or later.

Awkward Moment: Navigating the Uncomfortable Silence

So you've hit a conversational brick wall, and the silence feels deafening. Instead of blurting out the first thing that pops into your head out of sheer desperation, take a deep breath. Those brief silences can feel super awkward, and there's research to back it up. Studies show that even a tiny disruption in the flow of a conversation can make everyone feel uneasy and a bit rejected.[3]

On the flip side, fluent conversations give us social validation by creating a sense of consensus and agreement. So how do we get back into easy, breezy, flowy conversation mode? Here are a few tips.

Don't Blurt, Let It Trickle

According to Lisa B. Marshall, host of the podcast *Quick and Dirty Tips* and author of *Smart Talk: The Public Speaker's Guide to Success in Every Situation*, one way to avoid awkward silences is to make sure that you aren't blurting out all the possible connections between you and the person that you're speaking with all at once.[4]

Lisa shares an example of a postdoctoral student who had the chance to meet a world-renowned scientist she admired. Excitedly, the student rattled off all their shared connections in one breath, overwhelming the scientist and leading to an awkward silence. The lesson here? Pace yourself and let the conversation unfold naturally by mentioning one commonality at a time and then following it with an open-ended question.

Build an Emergency Kit of Topics

When you find yourself in a conversation lull, having a mental stash of go-to topics can be a lifesaver. Think of some interesting open-ended questions and conversation topics ahead of time to keep in your back pocket and break them out when needed. The questions should avoid controversial topics but also be engaging and lead to storytelling. For ideas, refer to Chapter 6 for ice-breaking questions you can add to your emergency kit.

End Your Answer with a Question

I'm cringing as I write this, just thinking about times when I've been in conversations with people who give short or yes/no answers to questions I ask. Don't be that person. Nobody likes to be the workhorse in a conversation. Be thoughtful in your response, drop clues for what to chat about next, and always end your response with an open-ended question to keep the conversation flowing. Have you ever noticed how much more engaging a conversation becomes when both people are genuinely curious and ask open-ended questions?

For example, instead of just saying, "Yes, I enjoyed the conference," you could respond with, "Yes, I really enjoyed the conference, especially the keynote speaker who talked about the future of AI. It was fascinating! What was your favorite part of the conference?" This way, you share something interesting and specific from your experience and invite the other person to do the same.

Know When It's Time to Go

Sometimes the conversation has just run its course. If the entire conversation is feeling forced and awkward, or it's clear that the lull is just signaling that the conversation is complete, it's perfectly okay to wrap things up gracefully. You don't have to stick it out until things get unbearably uncomfortable. A simple "It's been great chatting with you," or "I really enjoyed our conversation," followed by a natural exit strategy like one of the ones mentioned in Chapter 6, is all you need.

Remember, not every conversation will be a home run, and that's totally fine. You are not going to vibe with every single person you meet. You cannot please everyone; you aren't pizza, so don't sweat it and just carry on.

Awkward Moment: Forgetting Names

Let's be honest, we've all been there…standing in front of someone whose name just slipped through the cracks of your memory within the last five minutes. So, what do you do when you draw a blank?

While researching some strategies for handling this scenario, I came across so many sneaky ways to deal with this smoothly. But here's the thing: to truly be a no fear networker, you need to keep it real.

Instead of playing the guessing game or telling little white lies, why not just come clean? A simple "I'm sorry, I've just blanked on your name!" can actually turn into a moment of honesty that most people appreciate way more than a fumbled attempt to hide it. After all, who hasn't been there, right? Plus, it gives the other person a chance to feel good by helping you out – a win-win for rebuilding that connection.

So, keeping this in mind, here are some phrases you can use to ask the person for their name:

> *"Okay, this is embarrassing, but I've completely blanked on your name. Help me out?"*
>
> *"I'm great with faces, but names escape me like a squirrel in a dog park!"*
>
> *"I know we've met, and I remember our awesome chat about [topic discusses], but your name has just escaped me. What was it again?"*
>
> *"I'm blanking on your name, what was it again?"*

Let's also consider some ways to also make sure that you can forget names less:

1. **Give it your full attention:** When you're meeting someone, really make an effort to zone in on their name. It's good practice to see if you're actively listening!

2. **Repeat it back to them:** This one has worked so well for me. When they say, "Hi, I'm Charlie," you go, "Charlie, great to meet you!" It sounds crazy simple, but repeating their name out loud is like setting a mental bookmark for it.

3. **Use visual reminders:** According to Andrew Budson, a professor of neurology at Boston University and a lecturer in neurology at Harvard Medical School, the key to remembering names better is to use something in the person's appearance to remember them by. He explains, "For names beginning with 'V' like Victoria, look for a necklace or V-neck sweater and picture it as the first letter of their name. A pair of glasses held on their side looks like a 'B.' The lower lip and chin can form a 'D.' An ear can look like a 'G.' Sometimes patterns on clothing can form letters or give you other associations with names."[5]

4. **Practice it a few times:** Not only do people love to hear their own names, but it can also be super helpful to make it stick in your mind if you mention it a few times (naturally, don't be a weirdo) during a conversation. For me, I do this three times. I start the conversation by asking the person's name and making sure that I'm pronouncing it correctly by repeating it back to them. I try to use it in a question during the conversation, like, "What are your thoughts

on that, Anita?" and then I end the conversation by including their name, like this: "It was so nice chatting with you, Anita, have a great rest of your day!" Doing this not only makes the person feel valued and seen, but it also helps me remember their name for the next time that we meet or when I'm following up.

So, the next time you're sweating because someone's name has slipped your mind mid-convo, think about these tips. And remember, if all else fails, just pull out your phone with a smile and say, "I'd love to add you on LinkedIn. Could you help me out by typing your name? I'm far better at recognizing faces than remembering names!" We've all been there!

Awkward Moment: Saying the Wrong Thing

While interviewing people for this book, I reached out to an old acquaintance and left them a voicemail. My voicemails are generally...terrible. Whenever I'm put on the spot, I will almost inevitably fumble my words. This one was no exception. When I tried to explain the benefits of being interviewed for the book and the opportunities for cross-promotion, I accidentally blurted out "cross-pollination" instead. I sent him a follow-up message on LinkedIn explaining the mix-up and let him know to give me a call back whenever he isn't "buzzy."

I wish I could say this was a rare occurrence, but truthfully, I make silly slipups like this regularly. Years ago, when I was battling agoraphobia, a situation like that would have made me want to change my name and go off the grid completely, but now I try to take it in stride.

Unless you're a robot, mistakes during communication are bound to happen. The goal isn't to try and be perfect, although managing your social anxiety can be beneficial to reduce awkward flubs, but instead to learn how to deal with situations where you say the wrong thing. Here's what I do:

- **Acknowledge the slipup:** The first thing I do is just own up to it. Just like with the "cross-pollination" voicemail, I quickly acknowledge the mix-up. Most people appreciate honesty and can relate to the occasional word jumble.
- **Keep perspective:** Dr. Anthony Metivier points out[6] that thanks to something called inattentional blindness, most people barely register what we say. This means that even if you do trip over your words,

there's a good chance it wasn't even noticed. And even if it was, it's likely not as big a deal to the listener as it feels to you. Remembering this can help lessen the sting of embarrassment and keep the slipup in perspective. Also, we connect more with people who make the occasional error over the ones who seem too polished or perfect.

- **Apologize if necessary:** If you said something that might be taken offensively, make sure to quickly clarify what you meant and apologize in case it made a negative impact on your listener. You don't want hurt feelings to linger.

- **Learn from each mistake:** Every blunder is an opportunity to learn. What led to the mistake? Were you speaking too quickly? Did you not prepare enough? Were you nervous around the person? Reflecting on these questions can help you improve your communication skills for the future. Plus, being proactive about learning from these instances can turn them from mortifying to growth opportunities.

- **Give yourself grace:** Be kind to yourself. I used to beat myself up over every little mistake, but I've learned that this isn't healthy or even helpful. You can't be your confident, best, no fear networking self while carrying a backpack filled with shame and guilt. We all make mistakes, and showing yourself the same kindness you'd offer to someone else in your situation is crucial. This approach not only helps in coping with the current mistake but also builds resilience for future interactions.

So next time you say something you didn't mean to, remember that it's not the end of the world. It could even be the start of a more authentic connection!

Awkward Moment: Being Put on the Spot

There's nothing quite like the heart-pounding moment of being unexpectedly thrust into the limelight. Whether it's during a meeting when someone fires a tough question your way or during a conversation where you're suddenly asked to give your thoughts on a topic you know little about, being put on the spot can feel like being under a microscope.

But guess what? Even these cringeworthy moments can be handled with grace and a bit of quick thinking.

Here's how I've learned to navigate these tricky waters:

- **Take a breath:** When you're caught off guard, it's crucial to take a minute to breathe. This isn't just about filling your lungs; it's about pausing to let your brain catch up and engage fully. For me, this is particularly important if I sense from someone's body language that they might be trying to blindside me. A brief pause not only helps you collect your thoughts but also prevents that kneejerk reaction where you might say something you'll later regret. This small pause can be a powerful tool in maintaining your composure and ensuring your response is considered and concise.
- **Honesty is your ally:** If you don't know the answer or need more time to think about a response, there's no harm in being honest about it. Most people appreciate honesty and will respect your willingness to provide a thoughtful answer rather than making something up on the spot. Here are some ways to say more than just "I dunno" in a way that shows that you might not have the answer yet, but you're open to finding it.
  - "I'm not sure, but let me find out for you." This shows your willingness to help and ensures that you give the most accurate info.
  - "That's a great question; let me think about that and I'll get back to you." This compliments the question and shows your commitment to answering it.
  - "I'm not positive, but let's find out together." This approach shows humility, teamwork, and shared discovery.
  - "That's out of my area of expertise, but I know just the person to ask." Honest and resourcefully points them in the right direction.

Remember, there's power in admitting you don't have all the answers – it gives you a chance to level up your expertise. So next time you're stumped, just smile and confidently embrace the chance to learn something new!

- **Redirect the conversation or ask for more context:** If the spotlight is too intense, try redirecting the question to the group, or pivot to a related topic that you are more comfortable with. This can help alleviate the pressure while keeping the conversation flowing – for example, "I'm actually curious to hear everyone's thoughts on this. What do you think?"

Or sometimes you need to ask for more context to make sure you understand the question fully. Many times when I'm on stage and during Q&A, somebody asks a question that initially seems to be outside of my realm of knowledge, but when I ask for clarification, I get some context that makes it something I can totally answer with confidence.

Embracing these moments as opportunities to learn and stretch outside your comfort zone rather than pitfalls to fear can dramatically change how you handle being put on the spot. You're definitely not alone in feeling the heat; it happens to the best of us.

Hack Your Social Anxiety During Conversations

Becoming a no fear networker isn't about trying to banish your social anxiety completely; it's about learning how to manage it so you can engage confidently, about feeling the fear but doing it anyway. But that can be tough when your brain suddenly turns into Jello, your heart starts beating out of your chest, and the room starts spinning, right?

The key, then, isn't to just prep beforehand, get there early, and remember some awesome icebreakers, although all of those are important to make a good first impression. You also need to learn how your social anxiety manifests inside your body. For me, it feels like an alarm bell is going off. My vision gets fuzzy, my arms and hands start getting tingly, and I feel nauseous. Years ago, while battling agoraphobia, I would have these physical reactions pretty much anywhere there were people around: restaurants, banks, grocery stores, you name it.

Thankfully, these days my physical reactions to social interactions are much milder and more manageable. But I had to really tune into my body to learn to recognize those early warning signs before they escalated into a full-blown storm.

Once you start to notice those signs – maybe your breath quickens, or your palms get sweaty – it's good to have techniques ready to deploy to keep the conversation on track or be able to stay at an event without wanting to flee.

Here's how I've learned to hack my social anxiety in real time, sometimes even on stage in front of hundreds or thousands of people.

The Physiological Sigh

While simply taking a deep breath can help to calm your nerves quickly, there's another breathing technique, called the physiological sigh, that cranks it up a notch to get your confidence back on track. Developed by the brains at Stanford, including neurobiologist Andrew Huberman, this breathing technique is actually pretty easy.

Here's how to do it. First, breathe in deeply through your nose, and sneak in another quick, sharp breath to top it off. Then let it all out with a deep, sighing exhale. Doing this for about five minutes can not only help you to calm down but also is shown to have a positive effect on your mood. As Huberman points out in his YouTube video demonstrating this technique, it allows you to "feel more calm in real time, meaning without having to disengage from the stress-inducing activity."[7]

Sounds like the perfect breathing technique to try at your next event if you feel those butterflies in your stomach mid-conversation.

Sensory Grounding

One of the most effective ways that I've found to reduce my anxiety and even stop an anxiety attack in its tracks is with sensory grounding. Sensory grounding is tuning in to your surroundings to help anchor you back to the present when your nerves are carrying you away. It's about soaking in all the little details around you – the smell of your coffee, the sound of the fan whirring by the window – to bring you back down to a calmer state of mind.

There are many different grounding techniques, but the one I've found to be most beneficial is the 5-4-3-2-1 technique because it uses all of your senses and helps to snap you back to reality quickly. Let's pretend that you're mid-conversation with somebody at a coffee shop and suddenly you're feeling panic rising. Here's how you'd use this technique:

See: What are five different things you can see around you? Example: the menu board on the wall, a glass pastry display, the barista making a latte, the napkins in the middle of the table, the stainless steel espresso machine.

Touch: What are four things you can feel? Example: the rustic wooden surface of the table, the warm ceramic handle of your coffee mug, the metal button on your jacket, the plush chair you're sitting on.

Hear: What are three things you can hear? Example: the machines grinding coffee beans, the soft murmur of conversations around you, the clinking of the spoons against coffee mugs.

Smell: What are two things you can smell? Example: the freshly brewed coffee, the cinnamon buns baking in the oven.

Taste: What is one thing you can taste? Example: take a sip of your coffee, or if caffeine is your enemy at the moment, nibble on your slice of banana bread.

You can switch around the senses and numbers to whatever works best for you. The goal is to spend a moment truly taking in the things around you and remember that you are safe and everything, in this moment you're in, is okay.

Physical Anchors

In most of my social media posts and videos, you'll often spot me with a coffee mug in hand. This isn't just about my love for coffee; there's a deeper comfort attached to it. It's my physical anchor. No matter what has been going on in my life, there's one thing that I can almost always depend on. Every morning, no matter where I am in the world or what time zone I'm in, my delicious cup of coffee will be waiting for me.

For those of us with social anxiety, having a physical anchor like a coffee mug at an event can be a huge comfort. It provides a sense of stability and familiarity that can make all the difference. When you're at a networking event or even on a virtual meetup, holding onto something familiar can help manage anxiety levels. It's a little piece of home or comfort you can carry with you, grounding you amid the nerves.

Here are some other physical anchors you might consider if coffee isn't your thing:

Piece of jewelry: A bracelet, ring, or necklace that holds sentimental value can be a subtle yet powerful reminder of positive memories or supportive people.

A quote on your arm or hand: During stressful moments, a quick glance at your quote can serve as a reminder of what's important to you.

Lucky socks: Lucky socks are a discreet yet powerful anchor, like a cozy little hug for your feet, providing a hidden boost of confidence and a soothing touch that keeps you feeling safe and protected.

So if you find yourself feeling jittery or out of place, consider incorporating a physical anchor into your networking strategy. Whether it's a warm cup of coffee, a sentimental piece of jewelry, or even a pair of worn-out plaid socks, it can provide that touch back to confidence and calm your need to make meaningful connections.

Progressive Muscle Relaxation

One of the side effects of being in fight-or-flight mode is that your body tenses up, ready for rapid action. To help your body recognize that you aren't in physical danger by talking to Joe from accounting about the weekend, one way to relax your body is by tensing your muscle groups one by one and then relaxing them.

Obviously, mid-conversation, you're not likely to want to lie down on the floor for 15 minutes to do a full session of progressive muscle relaxation; however, you can still reap the benefits by simplifying it with a mini-muscle relaxation mid-conversation. For example, you can try clenching your fists under a table, and then releasing and stretching your fingers, or slightly lifting your shoulders and then letting them drop. If you're standing, you could also press your feet into the ground as hard as you can, and then release and relax your feet and calf muscles.

The key here is to figure out where you're holding the most tension in your body and try to give your body a gentle reminder that you're okay.

Handling Ruminations After the Event

You did it! You mustered up the courage, walked into that buzzing room, and mingled like a champ. But now you're back in the quiet comfort of your kitchen, nibbling on your favorite snack, and bam...it hits you. Your brain kicks into overdrive, replaying every single conversation. Did you laugh too loud? Was that comment about the weather too cliché? Did everyone notice that you have a bit of a stutter?

This post-event mental marathon is all too common, especially for those of us with social anxiety. As the evening silence deepens, our inner critics get louder, dissecting every detail.

Why You Ruminate

Rumination is like a broken record, except it's playing those cringeworthy moments on loop. It's our brain's way of processing social encounters, especially the bits where we think we messed up.

According to a recent study about rumination and social anxiety among Chinese students, those with social anxiety are more inclined to ruminate because of a cognitive bias that makes them focus more on negative information and potential threats in social situations.[8]

Let's examine what this might look like in action:

Omar, a college student, isn't exactly a big fan of the spotlight. In fact, he's taken as many of his classes virtually if possible. So the thought of today's class presentation is making the butterflies in his stomach do parkour.

As Omar slinks to the front of the class and clicks to his first slide, his eyes catch a couple of classmates whispering. Are they mocking him? Did he mess up the introduction?

Somebody else coughs and covers their mouth. Are they trying to cover up a laugh? Omar's mind is racing at this point.

He pushes through his presentation, but every yawn or blank stare is feeding his social anxiety. He's so focused on these potential negative reactions that he totally ignores the supportive nods and smiles from most of his classmates.

When it's finally over, instead of feeling relief and pride that he did something outside his comfort zone, he starts to spiral down the rabbit hole of ruminations. He replays every awkward pause and stumble, and his mind creates a blooper reel of a presentation that ends up getting an A+.

But the grade doesn't matter, because each perceived transgression feeds into the fear of future public speaking. Omar vows to avoid the spotlight again at all costs.

This scenario seems unreasonable when looking from the outside, and ruminations about awkward social interactions aren't generally rooted in reality. And what's more, just like in the example with Omar, these ruminations create a negative feedback loop, where social anxiety feeds into rumination, and then rumination feeds back into social anxiety. This can make it hard to break free from the merry-go-round of negative thoughts.

Fortunately, there are some helpful tools to rewire your thinking and redirect your rumination merry-go-round.

Schedule a Worry Window

A worry window is like scheduling a meeting with every worry you want to process post-events. Instead of letting your negative thoughts flood your brain, hit the snooze button on them and block out a time during your day, just 15–30 minutes, to reflect on the event and try to process any cringe-worthy moments that you need to.

This is something that I swear by. If I go to an event at night and then am lying in bed, starting to ruminate on everything that happened, I set an alarm on my phone for some time the next morning where I can dig into whatever is plaguing my mind. What's cool about this is that you are essentially training your brain to handle emotions on your terms, something that I didn't even think was possible until I started scheduling my rumination. Just make sure to keep it within the time space that you choose. Don't schedule a 15-minute session and wallow in worry for the next few hours. Stick to the window!

Validate and Redirect

I have a two-year-old daughter. Toddlers have very big emotions – I'm talking full meltdown over not being able to peel a pineapple like she can peel a banana. When the big feelings take over, my best strategy (besides finding a magical peelable pineapple) is to acknowledge her feelings and then redirect her attention to something else.

"I see you're disappointed that the pineapple won't peel like the banana does. We have a special cutter just for the pineapple, so do you want to see how I cut the pineapple? I can get your wooden knife so you can help me slice it too!"

On her podcast, *Happier with Gretchen Rubin*, Gretchen Rubin shares the advice to "treat yourself like a toddler," which basically means give yourself the same level of attention to needs and kindness that you would with a little kid.[9]

This feels especially true when dealing with rumination. Instead of trying to tell your brain to shut up or minimize how you're feeling, instead, validate your emotions: "I know you're feeling embarrassed about saying 'you too' when the Uber driver told you to have a safe flight home."

Follow it up by redirecting your focus onto an activity that will break you out of the mental loop. According to Dr. Alice Boynes, the activity you choose "should be an activity outside your wheelhouse, something you wouldn't usually do. An unusual-for-you activity will be absorbing and break you out of your thought process."[10] Fun activities could include assembling a puzzle, building with Legos, working out, playing a board or card game, or being adventurous with culinary experiments like trying a recipe you've never attempted before.

Engaging in these kinds of activities can provide a refreshing distraction from repetitive thoughts, leading to a mental reset. And as a personal touch, any activity that combines puzzles with the satisfaction of creating something delicious sounds great to me!

Understand the Spotlight Effect

I still remember the night before "dress down day" when I was in high school. I went to a Catholic school, so most of the school year I was forced to wear a white button-up shirt, black pants, and a forest green cardigan. Dress down days were a huge, monumental deal back then because it was the one Friday each month that you were allowed to dress in whatever you wanted (I mean, within reason).

So every month, my friends and I would go shopping at the mall, find the coolest ripped jeans and colorful tops, ready to make a fashion statement. Only this time, I had been sick and was forced to wear something I had – gasp – already worn!

I was pacing my room, trying to figure out what to do, when my mom came in and asked what was wrong. I told her, fully expecting her to share my horror, when she stopped me and said, "Mick, nobody is going to notice."

As a teenager, that one phrase made me seethe. Of course they would notice, how could they not?! But, over time, what felt like a major crisis in high school turned out to be one of the best lessons about the spotlight effect.

My mom was right. No one cared about my outfit as much as I did. The only comments that I got the next day were things like "Cool jeans!" or "Where'd you get your earrings?" That realization, that most people are too wrapped up in their own lives to scrutinize mine, was freeing. It taught me that the intense scrutiny I felt was mostly in my head.

The spotlight effect is pretty much exactly what it sounds like: it's believing that the spotlight is on you at all times and people notice, and scrutinize, your every move. It's the perception that you are the main character in a world where everybody also feels the same way about themselves.

So what does this have to do with rumination? Once you get that the spotlight effect is an overestimation of how much attention is being paid to you in every moment, you can start to chill about your own slipups. Chances are, people around you either didn't actually notice, or even if they did, it wasn't nearly as significant for them as it feels for you. For me, it's a huge relief to understand that the small details you obsess over likely go unnoticed, or barely registered by others.

So when you catch yourself starting to go down the rumination rabbit hole, remember the spotlight effect. This can help turn your obsessive catastrophic thoughts into just minor blips with a little more perspective.

As we wrap up this chapter, remember that networking isn't some mystical unicorn talent that only the lucky few are born with. It's a skill, pure and simple, one that you can totally master with a bit of practice. Think of each networking event as a chance to build on your social skills. You've got a whole toolkit now to help manage those butterflies and turn anxious moments into opportunities for real conversations that I know you can rock.

So next time you step into a room, remind yourself: this isn't just about making contacts; it's about making friends and learning as you go. If I can do it, I promise that you can too.

Overcoming
Setbacks

9 | Dealing with Rejection and Failure

Ever watch *Vanderpump Rules*? It's my all-time favorite guilty pleasure reality TV show. The series dives into the personal and professional lives of the current and former staff of Lisa Vanderpump's restaurants, who are entangled in a web of relationships, rivalries, and intense drama.

In a crazy turn of events, Tom and Ariana, once a solid couple and central figures on the show, are involved in a scandal where he cheats on Ariana with Raquel, another cast member and close friend of Ariana, leading to a fallout that ripples through their circle of friends. This creates an entirely charged atmosphere where social gatherings become battlegrounds of tension, judgment, and division.

Tom, post-scandal, tries to navigate social interactions with his group of friends amid a storm of whispers and judgment. His fear of being further ostracized by Ariana and their friends mirrors the heightened sensitivity to rejection that someone with social anxiety might feel. Every interaction is a potential threat; every casual glance might seem accusatory or dismissive. You can see in his interactions that he is constantly on guard, always on the defensive.

Ariana, dealing with intense feelings of betrayal and public scrutiny, must manage her interactions with Tom and mutual friends, balancing her hurt and the need to maintain her social standing within the group. She has to decipher every interaction that her closest friends are having with Tom, worry about whether she'll be cast aside in favor of him, and also try to manage her post-traumatic paranoia that stems from Tom cheating on her with her close friend. She scrutinizes every moment for new potential threats, while also putting on a protective shield to give off the "don't mess with me" vibes to avoid getting hurt again.

Now, what could this possibly have to do with networking with social anxiety? If you're a socially anxious person trying to network, every time you enter a social setting, it might feel like an episode of an explosive, emotionally charged reality show. Every interaction is magnified, every social cue is assessed, every introduction feels like an audition where you must prove your worth or be outcast from the group.

Fear of rejection is something that many, if not all, of us experience in social settings. However, studies have shown that people with social anxiety often show heightened rejection sensitivity and are more likely to anticipate, perceive, and be upset by rejection cues in social situations.[1]

Rejection sensitivity and social anxiety seem to make up a vicious cycle. Imagine you're at an event, chatting with somebody and you think the conversation is going well…until they start looking around the room, seemingly for an exit. "They hate me," you think, almost automatically. You end the chat abruptly and dash toward the door, feeling defeated and embarrassed for ever trying in the first place. The reality, of course, could be that the conversation actually was going well, but the person you were chatting with also has social anxiety and is just displaying a safety behavior (looking for an exit or averting eye contact), or they're waiting on a friend they were supposed to meet, or maybe they're battling a bout of explosive diarrhea and are actually scanning for the nearest restroom!

But your fear of rejection has already kicked into overdrive, and you feel both emotional and physical pain in your body. It hurts. And even as you start to feel better in the coming days and weeks, you still make a mental note of that painful feeling, and next time you're invited to an event, you decline out of fear that it will happen again.

Building Your Rejection Resilience

There is good news, though! Just as you can manage your social anxiety, you can increase your resilience to rejection.

Some of the best work that I've come across when it comes to building resilience when it comes to rejection comes from Jia Jiang, TED speaker and bestselling author of the book *Rejection Proof: How I Beat Fear and Became Invincible Through 100 Days of Rejection.*[2] He also happens to be a LinkedIn connection of mine!

Jia Jiang's road to becoming "rejection-proof" all started with a sting from his childhood:

> When I was six years old, my first-grade teacher...wanted us to experience receiving gifts but also learning the virtue of complimenting each other. So she had all of us come to the front of the classroom, and she bought all of us gifts and stacked them in the corner. And she said, "Why don't we just stand here and compliment each other? If you hear your name called, go and pick up your gift and sit down."
>
> Well, there were 40 of us to start with, and every time I heard someone's name called, I would give out the heartiest cheer. And then there were 20 people left, and 10 people left, and five left, and three left. And I was one of them. And the compliments stopped. Well, at that moment, I was crying. And the teacher was freaking out. She was like, "Hey, would anyone say anything nice about these people?....No one? Okay, why don't you go get your gift and sit down. So behave next year – someone might say something nice about you."[3]

This moment of public rejection leaves a lasting mark, planting a seed of fear of rejection that Jia carried with him into adulthood. Years later, he decided to take the brave leap into entrepreneurship, leaving the safety of a regular paycheck to chase his startup dreams. But then history repeated itself.

He faced a brutal rejection from a potential investor that felt just like the painful experience from his childhood, and it shook him to the core. Jia decided in that moment that he wouldn't surrender to his fear of rejection, and instead set out to build his rejection resilience and become "rejection proof" in 100 days.

Each day, he purposely sought out scenarios with a bunch of creatively outlandish requests where rejection was almost guaranteed. Some of these included asking a stranger if he could play soccer in their backyard, requesting a "burger refill" at a restaurant, and even asking to deliver the weather report on live TV.[4]

Each of these scenarios was designed to be unusual enough that rejection was the most likely outcome, allowing Jia to explore his reactions and the responses of others in these situations. What started as an experiment to increase his resilience toward rejection became something much more profound. He learned through the process that not only is rejection survivable, but opening yourself up to risk of rejection can open doors to cool opportunities that he never thought possible!

Here are some other lessons that we can learn from Jia's story.

Rejection Is Not Personal

One of the first things Jia realized during his experiment is that a lot of rejections have nothing to do with the person being rejected. It's often more about the rejector's own needs, preferences, or circumstances.

Psychologist and TED speaker Guy Winch says that in the aftermath of a rejection, though it may be tempting to beat yourself up, the assumption that rejection is personal is flawed. "Most rejections, whether romantic, professional, and even social, are due to 'fit' and circumstance. Going through an exhaustive search of your own deficiencies in an effort to understand why it didn't 'work out' is not only unnecessarily but misleading."[5]

So next time you face a no, remember that it's not a direct critique of you as a person but perhaps a sign that you're meant to be somewhere else, with someone else, or even something bigger. What seems like rejection may actually be redirection.

Asking "Why?" Opens Doors

As difficult as it was, whenever Jia faced a no he started asking why he was being rejected. This didn't just help him understand the other person's point of view, but sometimes it actually turned the no into a yes.

This reminds me of a time when I was rejected in person. Years ago, at the peak of my LinkedIn virality (go ahead, roll your eyes – I cringed even as I was writing that), I genuinely thought I had made it. From being jobless and relatively unknown to garnering millions of views on LinkedIn and seizing incredible opportunities, not to mention overcoming my agoraphobia, I felt utterly invincible.

Only there was one thing that I still dreamed of doing: speaking on stage for Social Media Marketing World, put on by Social Media Examiner, a publication I had admired since the beginning of my career. It's kind of like the Superbowl for social media marketing people. Prior to my first viral post on LinkedIn, I had applied to contribute. They rejected me and I never let it go.

So when momentum was on my side and I found myself invited to speak at VidCon, a massive conference in California, I was struck by a singular, overpowering mission: to track down Social Media Examiner CEO Mike Stelzner and prove my worth.

The moment I spotted him, I approached him with determination, sharing my achievements on LinkedIn and my dream to speak at his event. As I fantasized about the outfit I'd wear on stage, his response jolted me back to reality.

"You're not ready."

WTF?! Was he seriously rejecting me…again?! I was floored.

He gave me his business card and told me to email him. I dragged myself back to the airport like a wounded puppy, still trying to absorb the double rejection. I looked down at his business card.

Staring at his business card, the old me – the one who would have seen this as evidence that the world was too intimidating and rejection too unbearable – would have tossed it away, never to revisit the moment again.

But now I took it as something different. Maybe no actually meant not right now.

I emailed Mike. I asked why he had said no and asked how I could maybe turn it into a yes. He replied within minutes, giving me detailed instructions on how to show him I was ready for the opportunity.

It took me a year, but true to his word, after I completed my "homework" to get a yes, Mike reached out and invited me to speak at Social Media Marketing World in 2020, where I was ranked as a top speaker by attendees. None of it would have been possible if I had chalked up his rejection to personal flaws and tossed his business card instead of emailing him and asking why he had said no.

When I spoke to him recently about rejection and how people can get it to a yes, he said this: "When you study them and you understand what their mission is, you can position yourself in the way that you want them to perceive you, which can increase the likelihood that you will get a yes."[6]

Remember, every no holds a lesson. It's up to us to be curious, and leverage it to turn our next no into a resounding yes.

Persistence Pays Off

Jia found that sometimes just by not giving up at the first no and by coming back with a different angle or more information, people's responses changed. This persistence can be critical in overcoming rejections in your career or networking journey that might eventually become a yes.

Take Jack Ma, for example. Before founding Alibaba, one of the world's largest e-commerce platforms, he faced a staggering amount of rejection! Harvard turned him down 10 times, and he was the only one rejected among 24 applicants to KFC in his hometown, and over 30 different jobs turned him away.[7]

But instead of giving up, Ma saw each rejection as fuel, a push to keep moving forward. He believed deeply in the potential of the internet and used every "no" as a stepping stone, ultimately launching Alibaba. His persistence not only reshaped digital commerce in China but also made him one of the most respected business leaders in the world.

So remember, it's not just about the rejection, but whether or not you keep going. Who knows? Your next attempt might just be your own Alibaba.

Dealing with Failure and Bouncing Back

Failure is my least favorite F-word. Just writing it already conjures up moments where I've landed on my face. But here's the thing…those moments? They're not just stumbles; they're stepping stones to potentially something bigger and better.

I'm not here to sugarcoat the hard stuff. Feeling like you've failed freaking sucks. But while I'm happy to commiserate about the suckiness of it, we're also going to tackle it head on like true no fear networkers. We're going to break down what failure really is: a necessary pit stop on your journey, not the end of the road. I'll share insights on how to tackle setbacks headfirst, learn from them, and use them to launch yourself forward.

So saddle up, cowboys and cowgirls! We're about to turn those "why me?" moments into "watch me" opportunities. It's time to get into the hardest part of this networking thing.

Redefine and Reframe Failure

Let's get clear on something important: while failure is commonly defined in the dictionary[8] as a lack of success, there's a more critical aspect to it: the omission of a required action. That's the part we often overlook.

I'm going to be real with you here: networking is essential for career success. You cannot achieve all the cool things that you want to without connecting with others and building your network. Going out of your comfort zone is a required action; purposely avoiding discomfort is, by any standard definition, failure.

In his book *The Startup of You*, Reid Hoffman writes, "No matter how brilliant your mind or strategy, if you're playing a solo game, you'll always lose out to a team."[9] Networking is about building your team, your community. It's about creating connections that will push us beyond what we believe we're capable of alone.

Networking isn't always easy. Dragging yourself to an event when you'd rather curl up with a fuzzy blanket and scroll TikTok aimlessly can feel damn near impossible some days. And yes, you will probably mess up during social interactions. Maybe you accidentally call someone by the wrong name (I once did this three times; I was so nervous about messing it up again after the first time that it became like an ultra-cringy self-fulfilling prophecy), or your voice cracks like you've hit puberty just as you're pitching your big idea in a team meeting. Perhaps the room's energy is so intense that after just 30 minutes you feel the need to step out for a breather. But here's the twist: by simply showing up, you've already side-stepped real failure.

Still not ready to get out there because of your fear of failure? Try to think like an inventor. Thomas Edison was a master at flipping the script on failure. He once said, "I haven't failed; I've just found 1,000 ways that won't work."[10] What he meant was that each misfire wasn't a step back, but a step closer to the breakthrough he was ultimately chasing. Don't lose sight of your overall goal and try to reframe your failures as experiments that didn't work.

Turn Missteps into Material

If you truly want to turn those setbacks into stepping stones, these flubs, fumbles, and facepalms? They make freaking awesome stories. Here's a story about a failure of mine that I've shared on LinkedIn:

> *I cannot believe that after nine years of speaking on stages I was choking with stage fright again.*
>
> *I was so ready to share a post of that cool after shot, with the huge crowded room and me on stage, back in action after maternity leave.*
>
> *But right as I was about to press "post" a notification popped up.*
>
> *"Thank you for also sharing the hard stuff on LinkedIn"*
>
> *Well…crap. Here's what really went down.*
>
> *I was invited to speak in person for the first time since having a baby. I was thrilled, so excited to be back teaching people how to use LinkedIn.*
>
> *The organizers said it would be a big event, but nothing quite prepared me for that until I stepped into the room, with hundreds of people dressed in their best business attire, sipping their morning coffees.*
>
> *I excused myself to the washroom near the stage. "You got this, you've done this so many times before!"*
>
> *But the mirror affirmations weren't ringing true. I fussed with my hair, and worried that my outfit wasn't quite right. I stepped back outside, mentally obsessing over why I chose heels over flat shoes.*
>
> *"Please help me welcome our guest speaker, Michaela Alexis!"*
>
> *I climbed the stairs and stepped on stage. Okay, I made it.*
>
> *The screens…*
>
> *The screens were too far away. I couldn't see my slides.*
>
> *I couldn't see MY SLIDES.*
>
> *The crowds smiled sympathetically while I tried to map out my escape. My heart was beating so loud that I couldn't hear the words coming out of my mouth. I was having…stage fright. Just like my TEDx audition years ago.*
>
> *Maybe you've been there. So close up to your fear that you can feel its breath.*
>
> *Brené Brown once wrote, "vulnerability is not winning or losing; it's having the courage to show up when you can't control the outcome."*[11]
>
> *So, in that shaky moment. I took the deepest breath I could manage, stepped forward, squinted a few times, and found my footing. In the end, I had an awesome time speaking.*

> *And to everyone else who feels that tug of fear, remember...*
> *Your courage to show up, to try, and to be seen...is what makes your story (and not just the polished after shot) worth listening to.*

Sharing these moments on LinkedIn or at your next networking event can not only humanize you but can also make you more relatable.

Everyone loves a good comeback story or a laugh-at-yourself moment, and sharing a vulnerable story creates a space where deeper conversations can flourish. And who knows? Your next big opportunity might just come from someone who appreciates your candidness and courage to share the real, raw, sometimes messy journey of networking.

Find Lessons in the Stumble

I know this sounds a little woo-woo, but sometimes, by taking a moment to reflect, you may find lessons in that failure. Let's use the story of my slides as an example. I learned a few lessons from that experience that have made me a more prepared, confident speaker:

First, I should always do a practice run of the setup at events. Usually I will ask about things like presentation formats and microphones, but I never even thought to ask about how close the screens are to the stage. Knowing in advance would help me be more prepared by wearing my glasses or making special arrangements with the event staff in advance.

Second, I was able to recover! That is huge. My social anxiety used to be so crippling that once an anxiety attack started, there was no way I could continue. But because of the hard work I've done over the years learning how to better manage it, I was able to breathe through an anxiety attack on a huge stage with a spotlight on my face and continue the presentation and even enjoy it.

Third, this stumble made me rethink how I prepare for public speaking. It drove home the importance of always having a backup plan. Now I always keep extra notes and a printed copy of my presentation handy. No more relying solely on tech! Plus, I've started doing visualization exercises before I go on stage to mentally prepare for any hiccups.

This kind of preparation and mental readiness isn't just about avoiding future failures; it's about building resilience and confidence. Each time you stumble but recover, you're not just learning what to do next time, but you're learning that you can handle the unexpected. And that's something that extends far beyond public speaking. It's a life skill that turns catastrophes into mere bumps in the road.

Build a Setback Survival Kit

What do you do when you're feeling defeated? Maybe you take a walk and get some fresh air, watch a comfort show (mine's *Golden Girls*), or pour yourself a glass of wine and cocoon under your favorite blanket on the couch.

If you have a self-care routine that makes you feel a bit better, you'll love building a setback survival kit. Years ago I started putting together a little kit for those moments that just felt draining and overwhelming, when I just needed to press the pause button after a setback. Here's what I've included in my kit so you can steal some ideas to create your own:

- **Cheermergency contacts:** Pop a list in there of your go-to people who just get you. Whether it's a pep talk or just a quick giggle, make sure you've got your squad on speed dial.
- **Letter to yourself:** Write a letter to future you. Remind yourself of your strengths, your past victories, and the tough times you've navigated before. In it, be kind, be encouraging, and be honest. Future you will appreciate it so much. Here's an example of a letter you can use if writing isn't really your thing:

Dear Future Me,

If you're reading this, you're probably facing a tough day, and that's okay. Remember, even on the cloudiest days, the sun is still shining somewhere above. You've been through challenges before and have come out the other side stronger each time. Trust that this time is no different.

Think back to when you overcame [insert a personal past challenge here], how you felt, and the lessons learned. You've got a proven track record of grit, and this is just another opportunity to flex that muscle.

Remember to breathe deeply, stand tall, and approach the situation with the wisdom and grace you've gathered over the years. Allow yourself a moment of pause with a cup of tea and that favorite chocolate of yours (yes, it's there for exactly this reason).

Know that I believe in you deeply, and I'm proud of everything you've become and all that you are yet to achieve. Keep pushing forward with the courage I know you have, and don't forget to smile and remember your strength.

You are more capable than you realize. You got this.

- **Chocolate and tea bag:** Because, let's be real, chocolate and tea soothe the soul. Stash your favorite bar and a comforting tea blend to help calm down.
- **An encouraging book:** Throw in a book that fills you with courage and hope. (Mine is Cheryl Strayed's *Brave Enough*.) Sometimes a few powerful words are all it takes to turn your mindset around.
- **Tissues:** For those moments when you need to let it out, keep a packet handy to dry those tears.
- **Compliment cue cards:** Write some personal affirmations or have friends write out what they love about you. When you're feeling down, pull out a card and remind yourself of how amazing you are.

This kit isn't just about bouncing back; it's also about powering through with grace, humor, and a whole, whole lotta self-love. So next time life throws you a curveball, you'll be ready to catch it…with chocolate in one hand.

Don't Take It Personally

When you take failures personally, you see every setback as a direct reflection of your abilities or worth. Shame does nothing but keep you stuck. When you feel ashamed of your failures, it's not just about feeling sad or disappointed; it's about feeling fundamentally flawed. Brené Brown talks extensively about how shame can corrode the very part of us that believes we are capable of change.[12]

Shame wraps your failures around your identity, making it incredibly hard to move forward. Instead of learning from what happened, you might find yourself avoiding situations where you could fail again, which is poisonous for people like us already battling social anxiety.

So how do you move from taking it personally and feeling stuck in shame to understanding and growth? Start by recognizing your emotions and naming them. Are you feeling shame? Call it out. Are you taking something personally? Pinpoint why.

From there, look for objective facts and other perspectives. Reach out to mentors or friends who can provide a clear-eyed view of what happened.

By reflecting on the bigger picture, you may end up flipping the script a bit and considering the circumstances or environment impacting the situation. Maybe the market hasn't been good, the project expectations were as clear as mud, or you were just stressed with way more than usual.

Recognizing these outside players helps you handle things with more grace and keeps your self-esteem from taking an unnecessary hit. It's not always all on you; sometimes it's just the weather in the world around us.

By reshaping how you view failure, you can transform it into a powerful tool for personal development. Let's ditch the blame and shame game and step into a mindset that fosters grit and growth.

Celebrating Whisper Wins

Before we dive into the heart of celebrating whisper wins, let's take a moment to acknowledge a small yet mighty step you've already taken: you chose this book. You realized something wasn't working with your current networking game and decided it was time for a change. Choosing this book might feel like just another minor decision that you make every day, but trust me, it's the kind of choice that can create a ripple effect, armed with fresh insights and skills you didn't have before.

It's so important in networking, especially when you're socially anxious, to pause and toast to yourself along the journey. Acknowledging and celebrating the little milestones you hit helps to build both momentum to continue your growth, and also the confidence to keep going.

Whisper wins are those subtle, quieter victories that might not make the headlines but mean the world to you. If you decide to attend a networking event, and not only do you go, but you also initiate a conversation?! That's a whisper win. Or how about the times when you follow up with a new contact afterward asking for help on something despite the nagging fear of being seen as annoying? Huge whisper win!

So why do we sometimes fail to celebrate these wins? Often, it's because we feel shame that we aren't wired like our extroverted, social butterfly friends and coworkers. We deem our victories unworthy because they might not seem as challenging to others. But let's get one thing straight: your career journey is a solo adventure. You're not competing against anybody but yourself.

When you have social anxiety, just deciding to step into a room full of strangers can feel like your personal Everest. And just as we cheer for someone who has lost five pounds without dismissing it because it's not a hundred, or applaud someone who starts a daily walking routine without expecting a marathon, we should celebrate our personal feats no matter their scale.

Celebrating small wins also shifts your focus. How many times have you thought about how far you have to go versus how far you've come? Really think about that one for a minute. As humans, we're almost programmed to focus on what's ahead, what's next. However, taking stock of how far we've come is just as vital as planning our next steps.

A year ago, I was battling a massive postpartum hormone shift and recovering from a near-death experience during what was supposed to be a routine surgery. Those two factors collided and transformed into some of the worst anxiety I've ever experienced in my life. Setting small, achievable goals became my beacon through this storm.

Initially, my aim was simply to venture outside my home again, which I gradually managed with medical support, and then to extend my travels beyond Ottawa. After addressing a vitamin deficiency, I found new strength, leading me onto an international flight to Carpinteria, California, for a LinkedIn course recording – a task that had seemed totally out of reach forever.

The journey to Carpinteria was a struggle. I had a panic attack in the airport and another on the plane. But I eventually made it onto California soil and my recording was a success. On the last day of my work trip, I went to the nearby beach and sunk my toes into the sand. I turned my face toward the sunshine, tears welling in my eyes. I had made it. I had done the thing that just months earlier I was worried might never happen again.

So I encourage you to occasionally hit pause on your relentless pursuit and reflect on the things that the past version of you never thought possible. Celebrating these victories, big and small, is not just about acknowledging your progress; it's also about empowering yourself to face future challenges with resilience and grace.

Now here's a thought that might initially prompt a skeptical reaction, but stay with me: celebrating your own small victories genuinely transforms you into a more compassionate partner in networking.

Why? Because acknowledging your journey's challenges and victories deepens your empathy. When you take the time to honor your progress, you're not just patting yourself on the back – you're recognizing the effort, the setbacks, and the resilience it takes to move forward. This self-recognition fosters a profound sense of empathy within you.

This empathy naturally extends outward. You begin to see others' journeys through a more compassionate lens. Embarking on my networking journey, one of the most surprising benefits was the transformation in how I viewed others. Confession time: I used to be quite the impatient grouch in public settings.

"Why does this person take an eternity at checkout??" "Either move faster or step aside!" "Wow, you have a nice day too, buddy!" My inner narrative was a constant loop of how everyone else was inconsiderate, annoying, and downright rude.

However, something shifted when I began to tackle activities that pushed me out of my comfort zone to conquer my social anxiety. Gradually the world and the people in it started to appear in a different light. I noticed the cashier I previously thought was being slow on purpose had actually just been berated by a previous customer and was fighting back tears. It made me pause. Suddenly, the world didn't seem so black and white.

Then there was the time I found myself assisting an older customer at the self-checkout. They were struggling to scan items without barcodes, a task that was second nature to me but a challenge for them. This moment of helping someone navigate something new, recalling my own first-time experiences, made me grateful for this new softened perspective.

Getting into the habit of cheering for our own little victories teaches us to be the kind of understanding, patient people this world could really use a lot more of. So go ahead and lift that coffee mug high for every win, big or small.

10 | Conclusion

As we reach the final pages of this journey together, I thought about recapping all the strategies we've covered, but instead I want to speak straight from the heart, from one socially anxious professional to another.

I understand that the choices you're making are hard. Every room you enter, every hand you shake, every conversation you initiate – it's more than networking. It's a series of brave choices. You're not just reaching out to others; you're reaching deep, deep within yourself, pushing against the boundaries of your comfort zone.

You might not always feel it, but your efforts and courage are inspiring. You not only made the decision to try to grow despite your social anxiety, but you picked up this book and freaking read the whole damn thing. That's so powerful.

Remember, this journey is yours, and yours alone. It's about transforming your fears into stepping stones and saying to the world, "I'm here, my belly is rumbling with anxiety and I'm sweating through my jacket, but screw it, I'm here anyway!"

It's not only about finding new connections to add onto LinkedIn and awesome opportunities but also discovering new sides of yourself that you never knew existed that surprise you in the best possible way.

So keep reaching out, keep pushing through your worries, keep building those bridges. Every handshake, every smile, every "hello" is proof that you are more powerful than your fears. This book, as you hopefully see by now, isn't just about networking; it's about discovering and building the best version of perfectly imperfect you.

As for the book title, it may seem like a weird choice to simply try and tell you, the reader, "don't be afraid" (if it were only that easy, right?). It's kind of like when my husband tells me to "calm down" when I'm feeling anxious. Well meaning, sure, but not really realistic (and a bit infuriating).

No fear networking isn't about pretending your fears don't exist. It's about feeling that rush of anxiety and responding firmly, "Nope, you're not in charge here." As Brené Brown brilliantly puts it in *Daring Greatly*, "I will not let fear drive. Fear can ride, but it has to sit in the backseat."[1]

This book, with its bold title, is really about embracing that kind of bravery. It's about recognizing that you are much braver than you think, and stronger than you often feel. It's about not letting those nervous flutters stop you from moving forward, from reaching out, and from building a community of people who admire you in all your awkward glory.

So carry this message in your heart. Let it be a soft but firm whisper in those moments of doubt and anxiety: "Yes, I'm scared, but I'm not letting fear make my decisions for me anymore." That's the essence of no fear networking: not living without fear but living life beyond the white-knuckled grip of it.

As a reminder that we have more control over our destiny than we think we do, I want to leave you with a quote from an article I wrote as I personally navigated through the depths of my own social anxiety to where I am now:

> "Stop waiting for the tide to change. You are the tide. You have absolutely everything that you need to create the life you deserve. At some point, you'll need to decide whether to allow yourself to drift aimlessly and hope for the best, or strap on a life jacket and swim like hell towards the shoreline."

Social anxiety may make for a tougher swim, and the waves may feel overwhelming in rough seas, but I have no doubt that you'll soon be feeling the warm sand beneath your feet and will be smiling beside me.

Love and coffee, Mick

Appendix: Networking Resources and Tools

Your True North Traits Template

Introduction to True North Traits

As you develop your professional story, it's essential to move beyond just listing your skills. Consider what makes you uniquely you — your True North Traits. These traits encompass the innate talents, skills, and virtues that define your core identity and guide your professional path.

Discovering Your True North Traits

Talents:

When do I feel most authentic and true to myself? _____
_____

What activities cause me to lose track of time because I'm so engrossed? _____

What comes so naturally to me that others often struggle with it?

_____

In school, which subjects did I excel in without much effort?

_____

Skills:

What motivates me to get up in the morning with excitement?

_____

Which topics could I discuss endlessly without feeling tired?

_____

Reflecting on past challenges, which skills have I consistently relied upon? _____

When have I been the go-to person, and for what specific tasks or knowledge? _____

Virtues:

In what type of environments do I find myself thriving the most?

_____

What core values do I stand for, and how do they manifest in my life and work? _____

Which cause is so important to me that I would speak up about it passionately? _____

Who are my heroes and which traits do we share that inspire me?

_____

Crafting Your Professional Story

Who I Am:

Describe how your True North Traits shape who you are, beyond your job title: _____

Why I Do What I Do:

Explain how your inner compass has guided your career choices:

_____

How I Make a Difference:

Focus on the impact of your work, detailing how it serves others or affects the world: _____

What I Want to Do Next:

Share your future aspirations and how they connect to your True North Traits: _____

Final Touches:

Polish your narrative so it sounds natural and engaging, like sharing a story over coffee. Read it aloud to ensure it flows smoothly and authentically: _____

Networking Journal Template

Date: _____

Event Name: _____

Event Type: [Small meetup, large conference, virtual session, etc.]

Location: [Insert event location or platform]

Objective of Attending:

[Your goals for this event, e.g., meet potential clients, learn something new, find a mentor]

Preparation:

[Notes on how you prepared, e.g., researched attendees, prepared questions, practiced your pitch]

People Met:

Name:

Contact Info: [Email, LinkedIn profile]

Key Details: [Their role, company, potential opportunities]

Conversation Highlights: [Interesting tidbits, shared interests]

Follow-Up Actions: [Send thank you email, connect on LinkedIn, schedule follow-up meeting]

[Repeat as necessary for other contacts]

Comfort Level:

[How comfortable did you feel at the event on a scale of 1–10?]

[Specific aspects that affected your comfort level, e.g., crowd size, noise levels, venue]

Personal Insights:

[What did you learn about yourself?]

[Any triggers or anxiety moments?]

Event Feedback:

[What worked well? What could be improved?]

[Was the event aligned with your goals?]

Overall Reflection:

[Summary of the experience, total contacts made, potential opportunities]

[Would you attend this type of event again? Why or why not?]

Mood Tracker:

[Emoji or word to describe your mood post-event]

Additional Notes:

[Any other observations or thoughts post-event]

Notes

Chapter 1

1. American Psychiatric Association. *Diagnostic and Statistical Manual of Mental Disorders (5)*. Arlington, VA: American Psychiatric Publishing, 2013.
2. National Institute of Mental Health. (n.d.). *Social Anxiety Disorder: More Than Just Shyness*. Retrieved from https://www.nimh.nih.gov/health/publications/social-anxiety-disorder-more-than-just-shyness.
3. Social Anxiety Institute. (n.d.). *What is Social Anxiety?* Retrieved from https://socialanxietyinstitute.org/what-is-social-anxiety.
4. Ko, C.-Y. A., and Chang, Y. (2019). Investigating the relationships among resilience, social anxiety, and procrastination in a sample of college students. *Psychological Reports* 122(1): 231–245. https://doi.org/10.1177/0033294118755111.

Chapter 2

1. The Rolling Stones (1969). You Can't Always Get What You Want, *Let It Bleed*, Decca Records.
2. Hendriksen, E. (2018). *How to Be Yourself: Quiet Your Inner Critic and Rise Above Social Anxiety*. New York: St. Martin's Press.
3. Cokley, K. et al. (2019). Imposter syndrome among racial and ethnic minority college students: the role of anxiety, academic self-concept, and racial microaggressions. *Clinical Psychological Science* 8(5): 715–731.

4. Rosa, C. (2018). Emma stone opens up about her first panic attack, *Glamour*. https://www.glamour.com/story/emma-stone-opens-up-about-first-panic-attack. (1 October 2018).

5. ABC News (2005). Barbra Streisand looks back on 25 Years. *ABC News*. https://abcnews.go.com/Primetime/Entertainment/story?id=114 7020&page=1 (21 September 2005).

6. Osaka, N. (2021). Twitter post. https://twitter.com/naomiosaka/status/ 1399404243170074625 (31 May 2021).

7. Osaka, N. (2022). Quoted in Alexandra Schonfeld. Naomi Osaka Says She's Having 'a Blast' on Tennis Court for 'First Time in a While', *People*. https://people.com/sports/naomi-osaka-says-shes-having-a-blast-on-tennis-court-for-first-time-in-a-while/ (9 May 2022).

8. Rhimes, S. (2015). *Year of Yes: How to Dance It Out, Stand in the Sun, and Be Your Own Person*. New York: Simon & Schuster.

9. Schroeder, A. (2008). *The Snowball: Warren Buffett and the Business of Life*. New York: Bantam Books.

10. Gandhi, M.K. (1957). *The Story of My Experiments with Truth: An Autobi ography*. Boston: Beacon Press.

Chapter 3

1. American Psychological Association. Safety behavior, *APA Dictionary of Psychology*, https://dictionary.apa.org/safety-behavior (accessed 21 June 2024).

2. Hott, R. Unpacking social anxiety. *Psychwire*. https://psychwire.com/ free-resources/q-and-a/12t3yk3/unpacking-social-anxiety (accessed 21 June 2024).

3. Hendriksen, E. Unpacking social anxiety. *Psychwire*. https://psychwire .com/free-resources/q-and-a/12t3yk3/unpacking-social-anxiety (accessed 21 June 2024).

4. Anxiety Canada. Social anxiety in adults. https://www.anxietycanada .com/disorders/social-anxiety-in-adults/ (accessed 21 June 2024).

5. Google. Networking. Accessed 21 June 2024.

6. Brown, B. (2012). *Daring Greatly: How the Courage to Be Vulnerable Transforms the Way We Live, Love, Parent, and Lead*. New York: Gotham Books, p. 34.

7. Ibid, p. 45.
8. Roberts, A. interview with author, 12 April 2024.
9. Robin, C. email message to author, 14 June 2024.

Chapter 4

1. Ottawa's most boring city reputation. *CBC News,* https://www.cbc.ca/player/play/1.7038243 (accessed 24 June 2024).
2. Cuncic, A. What is imposter syndrome? *Verywell Mind,* https://www.verywellmind.com/imposter-syndrome-and-social-anxiety-disorder-4156469 (accessed 24 June 2024).
3. Boonchan, S., Kasirawat, C., Khunanon, P. et al. (2023). Exploring factors affecting impostor syndrome among undergraduate clinical medical students at Chiang Mai University, Thailand: a cross-sectional study, *Behaviorial Sciences* 13(12). https://doi.org/10.3390/bs13120976.
4. Bravata, D.M., Watts, S.A., Keefer, A.L. et al. (2020). Prevalence, predictors, and treatment of impostor syndrome: a systematic review. *Journal of General Internal Medicine* 35(4): 252–1275, 10.1007/s11606-019-05364-1.
5. Wilson, S. (2018). *First, We Make the Beast Beautiful: A New Journey Through Anxiety.* New York: Dey Street Books.
6. Angelou, M. As quoted in The Academy of Achievement. https://achievement.org/achiever/maya-angelou (accessed 24 June 2024).
7. Mohr, C. and Jonauskaite, D. (2020). Cross-cultural comparison of color-emotion associations. *Journal of Cross-Cultural Psychology* 51(4): 467–478, 10.1177/0022022119889634.

Chapter 5

1. Mershon, P. interview by author, Zoom, 21 March 2024.
2. Hendriksen, E. (2018). *How to Be Yourself: Quiet Your Inner Critic and Rise Above Social Anxiety.* St. Martin's Press, p. 24.
3. American Psychological Association, *APA Dictionary of Psychology,* Introversion.
4. Phimmasene, K. et al. (2023). Sociality and motivation: women's affiliative trends throughout the menstrual cycle. *Psychoneuroendocrinology* 152. https://doi.org/10.1016/j.psyneuen.2023.106203.

5. Grant, A. Quiz: are you an extrovert, introvert or ambivert? *TED IIdeas*. https://ideas.ted.com/quiz-are-you-an-extrovert-introvert-or-ambivert/ (accessed June 24, 2024).

6. Handley, A. personal communication, 26 July 2024.

7. Deziel, M. Interview by author, Zoom, 25 March 2024.

8. Casciaro, T., Gino, F. and Kouchaki, M. (2014). The contaminating effects of building instrumental ties: how networking can make us feel dirty. *Administrative Science Quarterly* 59(4): 705–735.

Chapter 6

1. Davis, J.A. How do you feel about Small Talk? How can we make it better? *TikTok*. https://www.tiktok.com/@jeremyandrewdavis/video/7213787101740010798 (accessed 27 June 2024).

2. "Small talk," *Oxford Dictionaries* definition, cited in "Why Small Talk Is a Big Deal," *Psychology Today*. https://www.psychologytoday.com/ca/blog/out-the-ooze/202001/why-small-talk-is-big-deal#:~=Small%20talk%20is%20defined%20by,engaged%20in%20on%20social%20occasions (accessed 27 June 2024).

3. Chitchat and Small Talk Could Serve Evolutionary Need to Bond with Others, Princeton University, 14 December 2015. https://www.princeton.edu/news/2015/12/14/chitchat-and-small-talk-could-serve-evolutionary-need-bond-others (accessed 27 June 2024).

4. Relational Diversity in Social Portfolios Predicts Well-Being, Harvard Business School. https://www.hbs.edu/ris/Publication%20Files/Relational%20Diversity%20in%20Social%20Portfolios%20Predicts%20Well%20Being_d606bf1c-4c59-411c-84f0-f8dca0cebcad.pdf (accessed date 27 June 2024).

5. Cuddy, A. Your body language may shape who you are. *TED Talk*. https://www.ted.com/talks/amy_cuddy_your_body_language_may_shape_who_you_are?utm_campaign=tedspread&utm_medium=referral&utm_source=tedcomshare (accessed 27 June 2024).

6. Casciaro, T., Gino, F. and Kouchaki, M. (2015). The contaminating effects of building instrumental ties: how networking can make us feel dirty. *Administrative Science Quarterly* 60(4): 705–735, 10.1177/0001839214554990.

7. Hall, J. Conversation with the author, followed by email, June 2024.

8. Robin, C. (2021). *Connect: Building Exceptional Relationships with Family, Friends, and Colleagues.* New York: Currency.
9. Julian Treasure, Communication Means Paying Attention: The Four Pillars of Active Listening, Stanford Graduate School of Business Insights. https://www.gsb.stanford.edu/insights/communication-means-paying-attention-four-pillars-active-listening (accessed 3 July 2024).
10. Cuncic, A. *The Anxiety Workbook*, description of techniques for improving eye contact, accessed 3 July 2024.
11. Voss, C. (2016). *Never Split the Difference: Negotiating as If Your Life Depended on It.* Harper Business, p. 53, discussion on mirroring technique.
12. Mulholland, R. Email communication regarding the dynamics of networking and social interactions at events, 7 May 2024.
13. Ruan, C. How to end a conversation according to psychologists, *Parade.* https://parade.com/living/how-to-end-a-conversation-according-to-psychologists (accessed 3 July 2024).
14. Quirk, B. (2023). Women need to feel good about themselves. *Capital Times*, Madison, Wisconsin, 22 July 2003, p. 4D.

Chapter 7

1. Brown, B. (2012). *Daring Greatly: How the Courage to Be Vulnerable Transforms the Way We Live, Love, Parent, and Lead.* Gotham Books.
2. Roosevelt, T. Citizenship in a Republic, speech delivered at the Sorbonne, Paris, 23 April 1910.

Chapter 8

1. How Communication Works, How to Join a Conversation: When to Talk (Communication Training), YouTube. https://youtu.be/hkCUoQNeBX0?si=zI_rSVZ22wccTQY8 (11 June 2018).
2. Robbins, M. (2020). Psychological Tricks to Boost Your Influence, Income, and Impact Today! *The Mel Robbins Podcase,* YouTube. https://youtu.be/FVmTeH0uK5k?si=qfYAqRO4BvP6Atv3.
3. Green, R.L. and Adams, A.B. (2011). Stress and openness to interracial interactions. *Journal of Experimental Social Psychology* 47(1): 123–128.

4. Marshall, L.B. 5 Tips that'll help you avoid that dreaded awkward silence, *The Muse*, 19 June 2020. https://www.themuse.com/advice/5-tips-thatll-help-you-avoid-that-dreaded-awkward-silence.

5. Budson, A.E., How to remember names, *Psychology Today*, July 2018, https://www.psychologytoday.com/ca/blog/managing-your-memory/201807/how-to-remember-names.

6. Metivier, A. How to stop punishing yourself when you say stupid things. *Magnetic Memory Method*. https://www.magneticmemorymethod.com/how-to-stop-punishing-yourself-when-you-say-stupid-things (accessed 24 June 2024).

7. Huberman, A. Breathing techniques to reduce stress and anxiety: Dr. Andres Huberman on the physiological sigh, YouTube video, 9:15, https://www.youtube.com/watch?v=kSZKIupBUuc (18 July 2023).

8. Wu, P. et al. (2024). Cross-lagged analysis of rumination and social anxiety among Chinese college students. *BMC Psychology* 12(1): 1–10. https://doi.org/10.1186/s40359-023-01515-6.

9. Rubin, G. *Happier with Gretchen Rubin*, episode 7: Treat Yourself Like a Toddler. https://gretchenrubin.com/podcast-episode/podcast-7-treat-yourself-like-a-toddler/ (accessed 24 June 2024).

10. Boyes, A. How to break free from negative thinking. *Psychology Today*. https://www.psychologytoday.com/us/blog/in-practice/202002/how-break-free-negative-thinking (12 February 2020).

Chapter 9

1. Winch, G. (2014). *Emotional First Aid: Healing Rejection, Guilt, Failure, and Other Everyday Hurts*. New York: Plume, p. 45.

2. Jiang, J. (2015). *Rejection Proof: How I Beat Fear and Became Invincible Through 100 Days of Rejection*. New York: Harmony.

3. Jiang, J. What I learned from 100 days of rejection. *TED Talk*. https://www.ted.com/talks/jia_jiang_what_i_learned_from_100_days_of_rejection (February 2015).

4. Jiang, *Rejection Proof*, pp. 15–18.

5. Winch, G. *Why Rejection Hurts So Much – and What to Do About It*, TEDx Linnaeus University. https://www.ted.com/talks/guy_winch_why_rejection_hurts_so_much_and_what_to_do_about_it (April 2014).

6. Stelzner, M. Personal interview, 10 May 2024.

7. Jack Ma: From 'Rejected' to Billionaire, *Forbes*. https://www.forbes .com/sites/russellflannery/2015/05/06/jack-ma-from-rejected-to-billionaire/?sh=1893a6b31c2c (accessed 24 June 2024).

8. Failure, *Merriam-Webster*. https://www.merriam-webster.com/ dictionary/failure (accessed 24 June 2024).

9. Hoffman, R. and Casnocha, B. (2012). *The Startup of You: Adapt to the Future, Invest in Yourself, and Transform Your Career*. New York: Crown Business, p. 83.

10. Edison, T. (2007). As quoted in *The Book of Positive Quotations* by John Cook, Steve Deger, and Leslie Ann Gibson. Minneapolis: Fairview Press, p. 146.

11. Brown, B. (2012). *Daring Greatly: How the Courage to Be Vulnerable Transforms the Way We Live, Love, Parent, and Lead*. New York: Gotham Books, p. 2.

12. Ibid.

Chapter 10

1. Brown, B. (2012). *Daring Greatly: How the Courage to Be Vulnerable Transforms the Way We Live, Love, Parent, and Lead*. New York: Gotham Books, p. 36.

Acknowledgments

This book would not have been possible without the support, wisdom, and encouragement from a remarkable group of people. My deepest thanks go to Christina Rudloff, my acquisitions editor at Wiley, who believed in this project from the start and championed my vision, and Purvi Patel and Deborah Schindler, my managing editors, who kept me on track and focused. To Wiley, for taking a chance on a socially anxious, awkward, LinkedIn-obsessed networker with a story to tell – thank you for making this possible.

Massive thanks to Julie Kerr, my developmental editor, for your guidance and wisdom in shaping this manuscript. And to the brilliant minds like Rich Mulholland, Mike Stelzner, Phil Mershon, April Roberts, Melanie Deziel, John Hall, and Dr. Carole Robin – your insights sparked so many lightbulb moments and deeply enriched this project.

A heartfelt thank you to my husband, Ryan, who never let me doubt this journey, and to my girlfriends, who helped me nail that cover design! Also, a giant thank you to everyone who privately messaged me on social media to share their personal battles with social anxiety; your stories inspire and drive me, and I'm honored that you chose to share them with me.

I must also acknowledge the pioneers in the mental health space like Brené Brown, Cheryl Strayed, Glennon Doyle, and Elizabeth Gilbert. Your work has opened doors and made it safer for all of us to discuss the challenges we face without fear of judgment. Similarly, a special thanks to communication experts Ann Handley and Carmine Gallo, whose work in written and spoken communication continues to inspire me.

And finally, to you, the reader, for giving me your time, life's greatest resource. I hope this book helps you to find what you're seeking.

About the Author

Hailing from Ottawa, Canada, Michaela Alexis, known to her friends and followers as Mick, is currently one of North America's most renowned speakers on LinkedIn-related topics. Her journey began in 2016 when an article she wrote about landing her dream job went viral on LinkedIn. Since then, she's replicated that success with dozens of articles receiving millions of reads, and featured on platforms like CNBC, *The New York Times*, Buzzfeed, and *Inc.*

Over the past decade, Mick has managed the online presence of more than 100 businesses worldwide, partnered on and starred in brand campaigns with Crowne Plaza Hotels and K-Swiss, and built a vibrant LinkedIn community of over 200,000 followers. She coauthored the book *Think Video: Smart Video Marketing and #Influencing* and is an official LinkedIn Learning Instructor with three popular courses on LinkedIn marketing and social media copywriting.

But Mick's journey hasn't been without its challenges. In her 20s, she battled agoraphobia, a condition that kept her housebound and fearful of the outside world. Through sheer determination and resilience, she not only conquered this challenge but also transformed it into a source of inspiration, becoming an international speaker and trainer. Her remarkable story fuels her mission to empower others to overcome the profound barriers of extreme social anxiety.

Away from the buzz of LinkedIn tutorials and client sessions, Mick revels in life's quieter moments with her husband, Ryan; their wild toddler, Isla; and their trio of dogs, Kennedy, Cooper, and Koa. A devoted coffee lover to her core, Mick finds joy in crafting engaging stories, her creativity often fueled by the comforting smell (and caffeine) of a freshly brewed cup of coffee.

Index